WORLD CUP
USA '94

The Complete Guide to Soccer's World Cup and All 24 Teams

WORLD CUP USA '94

Glen Phillips and Tim Oldham

CollinsWillow
An Imprint of HarperCollins*Publishers*

First published in 1994 by
HarperCollins*Publishers*
10 East 53rd Street
New York, NY 10022

This edition published in 1994 by Collins Willow
an imprint of HarperCollins*Publishers*, London

A CIP catalogue record for this book is
available from the British Library.

ISBN 0 00 218485 0

Printed in Great Britain

CONTENTS

INTRODUCTION

The United States is about to witness an invasion on an unprecedented scale. For one month during the summer of 1994 the eyes of the world will be focused on the soccer World Cup finals. Not even the Olympic Games generate such passionate interest around the world. Every goal, every save, and every incident will be discussed, debated, praised, and criticized as soccer fans everywhere turn their attention to the action in the United States.

The World Cup is no ordinary soccer tournament. It decides the champions of the world—the team that will follow in the illustrious footsteps of Germany, Brazil, Argentina, Uruguay, Italy, and England, the only teams ever to have won the ultimate accolade in sport.

National pride is at stake and the players from each team know that they carry the hopes of their country with them. Each team and player will have their own aspirations. For some teams, like Greece, just getting to the finals has been a great achievement while for others, like Italy and Germany, failure to reach the semifinals will be considered a disaster. But beyond winning or losing, the tournament is a celebration of the world's most popular sport.

This year has the makings of a great World Cup. Much centers around the performances of a few key players. Every tournament has seen a great player come to the forefront and dominate the world stage. Pele, Eusebio,

Cruyff, Platini, and Maradona have all left their mark on the competition, but whose turn is it now? Italy's Roberto Baggio is the heir apparent but Romario of Brazil, Andy Moller of Germany, and Dennis Bergkamp of Holland all have the individual flair and the ability to stake their claim as the world's best. This is their opportunity.

Though one player can make a good team great, soccer is a team sport and the eventual champions will be expected to win seven games against top opposition before being crowned world champions. While no team stands out as an overwhelming favorite, one must always respect the defending champions, Germany. Colombia, too, is one of the most attractive international teams and they have high expectations of making significant progress. Winning the World Cup is a national obsession, too, for everyone involved in Brazilian football and Italy's fervent supporters will be equally committed to their team's success.

Argentina, another traditional giant of world soccer will also be present, but there are several countries new to the finals. One of these, Nigeria, may cause some surprises. It is widely believed that Africa will produce a World Cup–winning team in the near future. But is this the year? Probably not, but Nigeria and Cameroon will be entertaining teams to watch.

And what of the host nation? Written off by many pundits, the United States team has a lot to prove and has drawn a difficult opening group. But the players are not lacking commitment and preparation. If there is some individual flair and if the American people get behind their team, the players could raise their game and do themselves and their country proud.

It is going to be a great tournament and we hope that this guide will provide you with all the facts and figures to help you enjoy this wonderful competition to the full.

ORIGINS:
HOW IT ALL BEGAN

It is beyond doubt that soccer is the most popular game on earth. More than 170 nations are affiliated with the *Federation Internationale de Football Association* (FIFA), and even the United Nations cannot boast such an impressive membership. It was estimated by FIFA that 2.7 billion television viewers, half the population of the world, watched the 1990 World Cup finals in Italy.

But figures alone cannot do justice to the game. They cannot capture the history or tradition. They cannot convey the jubiliation of victory or the despair of defeat, nor do they reflect the aspirations of children who dream of playing with the artistry and skill of the great players. In short, soccer, in one form or other, has had a profound effect on the culture of our planet. Hey!—it's that important.

The formation of the Football Association (FA) in a London tavern on October 26, 1863, was the first milestone in the history of organized soccer. Before then it was a confused and chaotic pastime, and it required great courage and inspiration from the FA to inject a sense of order and provide shape, momentum, and direction to the game. From these humble beginnings sprung the shoots of the game as we know it today: the game's laws, league soccer, coaching, professionalism, cup competitions, a code of conduct.

But if the game developed primarily in England, that country cannot be described as its birthplace. As soon as an ancient Greek or Egyptian first kicked, bounced, or passed an object to a companion, the seeds of soccer had surely been sown. Once the "game" had been adapted to include a ball, all the principles of the modern game were established: a conflict where one set of combatants tries to force the ball through the territory to the target of an opposing group. It is as simple as that whether it is American, Association, Gaelic, Australian Rules, or Rugby football. The beauty is in its simplicity.

It is not surprising, therefore, to find considerable evidence suggesting that the game grew at numerous points around the world quite independently. Nearly 2,000 years ago, the Chinese of the Han Dynasty played a sort of target soccer they called *tsu chu* which is translated as "kick ball." On the emperor's birthday, two long bamboo poles were set up in front of the palace and a silk netting stretched between. Rival teams would attempt to kick a ball through a small circular opening cut into the netting, a feat that required considerable skill. The Japanese devised a game called *kemari* that involved eight participants who passed a ball to one another within a square area. At each corner of the square stood a different kind of tree: a pine, a willow, a maple, and a cherry tree. *Kemari* was an elegant, ritual performance with religious significance; hence the setting amid these symbols, each of which was held as sacred.

The Romans adapted a Greek ball game that spread rapidly through their Empire under the name of *harpastum*.

This was played on a rectangular field between two teams who defended the lines that marked the ends of the field. There was also a center line. The object of this game was to throw the ball from player to player, moving forward all the time, and eventually to throw it over the opponents' line.

Harpastum was by no means the only ball game played by the Romans, but when they occupied Britain, it is almost certain that they encouraged the game. According to legend, the first game played among the Anglo-Saxons was a victory celebration, using the severed head of a defeated Dane as a ball. The story has been discredited by some but the tribal element of the game is nicely encapsulated.

British soccer evolved in a form that was barely to change for 1,500 years. It was little more than an excuse for a riot, a ferocious cross-country village game or violent activity of the streets and marketplaces. Games would set town against town, often with hundreds of participants on each side, with "goals" that might be several miles apart.

Several monarchs, including Edward III, Richard II, and Henry IV, attempted to ban the game, as they were concerned that soccer was bad training for battle and got in the way of regular archery practice. The game was banned time and again in England and Scotland without any lasting effect. Here was the strong, if somewhat primitive, seed of the world game. The next stage in its development was possibly the most important.

The early 19th century saw an upsurge in the interest in education. It was the public school era in England and, denied the opportunity to take part in their normal pastimes such as riding, hunting, and fishing, the boys quickly adapted the principles of the rough town-and-village games to the schoolyard and playing field. A sense of purpose was detected, and a few forward-thinking teachers accepted the idea of organized games and actually encouraged boys to play soccer.

The schools developed their own styles of soccer and although it was difficult, if not impossible, for one to play another, the game became part of the tradition of each school. At Charterhouse, twenty-a-side matches were played where long kicks, passing forward, and handling were not allowed, and dribbling the ball was the order of the day. At Harrow, the field was comparatively big, and high kicking and catching the ball were encouraged—although carrying the ball was disallowed. At Eton, the Wall Game was played on a pitch 120 yards long and just 6 yards wide. And at Rugby, too, soccer was a wide-running game with handling allowed—until one summer in 1823, when William Webb Ellis picked up the ball and ran with it. The rules forbade advancing the ball in any way except kicking it, but Rugby School decided to accept the practice into their rules. Rugby went one way and the other schools another. Ellis's innovation became the basis of rugby, a game that would influence American football because the runner could carry the ball as well as kick it.

THE DEVELOPMENT OF RUGBY AND AMERICAN FOOTBALL

● ● ● ● ● ● ● ● ● ● ● ● ● ● ● ● ● ● ● ●

The birth of American football has its roots in soccer and rugby. When William Webb Ellis picked up the ball and ran with it at Rugby School in 1823 most people were outraged. Little did they suspect the long-term significance of his actions.

Throughout the 1850s and 1860s, soccer and rugby both became popular in the United States. On November 6, 1869, Rutgers and Princeton played what is officially considered the first American college football game, although it used rules more like those of Association soccer than modern American football. Each team had 25 players, the ball was advanced by kicking or heading, and the goal posts were 25 yards apart.

Over the next seven years, different schools played with slightly different rules until, at the Massasoit Convention, the first rules were written to unify the game. In the next decade, under the careful guidance of Walter Camp of Yale—the man who became accepted as the father of American football—the game adopted the rules finally distinguished it from soccer or rugby.

Camp persuaded his associates to limit the teams to 11 a side. The scrum was replaced by the center's snap to the quarterback. Two years later, Camp created the system of downs, in which a team needed to gain five yards in three plays or lose the ball. This inspired the first prearranged play strategy and spoken signals. In 1883 point values were set, and two years later the first referees were appointed to assess penalties.

● ●

While the boys were still at school, the differences in the rules of the game hardly mattered, but when the players moved from school to university, confusion reigned. Everyone now wanted to play soccer, but under which rules? It was clear that if they were to continue playing, a universal set of rules acceptable to everyone would have to be drawn up.

The first move toward unification came in 1848 and

was made by a group of 14 men from Cambridge who represented the schools of Eton, Harrow, Winchester, Rugby, and Shrewsbury. They drew up what became known as the Cambridge Rules—rules that were adapted and refined in the 1850s. Goals were awarded for balls kicked between the flag posts and under the string; goal kicks and throw-ins were given much as today; catching the ball direct from the foot was allowed providing the catcher kicked it immediately and there was no "out of play" movement in front of the ball—an early definition of the offside rule.

The game was now established on a common foundation, and amongst all the inter-university and inter-school games arose the first recognizable soccer clubs. After their studies, graduates from universities carried their enthusiasm for the game to the outside world, and it wasn't long before a group working in Yorkshire founded the Sheffield Cricket and Football Club in 1855. As in Sheffield, so in other places soccer clubs were started, and by 1863 yet another attempt was made to formulate a universal code of rules.

Representatives of the leading clubs met at the Freemason's Tavern in Great Queen Street in London on October 26, where it was decided that the body should be known as the Football Association. They had achieved an important goal—the formation of an authority that they hoped would lead to the unification of what was still a hopelessly fragmented game. They were aware of their responsibilities and also of the potential of the game. The early meetings were stormy and led to bitter wranglings and divisions, but they persevered.

The game, they agreed, would be a combination of handling and dribbling. Every player would be able to handle the ball and when he caught it he "made a mark" with his heel and so won a free kick. But the friction between the members who supported the rugby code and those who favored the dribbling code worsened. The issue that eventually prompted rugby to go its separate way was that of hacking, or kicking an opponent on the leg. Rugby men felt it was a manly feature of the game and showed character, whereas advocates of the dribbling game considered it vicious. The rift was never healed, and after accusing the others of being cowards, the Rugby men walked out of the FA.

The FA was now united in purpose, and over the next two years all the distinctive features of rugby were rejected. Early in 1866 the powerful Sheffield club, the oldest and most influential club, suggested that a match should be played between the clubs of London and Sheffield. The game was played on March 31 and won comfortably by London with the first goal fittingly being scored by E. C. Morley, the secretary of the FA. Other matches quickly followed, and by as early as 1872 England and Scotland were playing internationals and the FA Cup had started its glamorous career.

Soccer had been growing and developing as a form of entertainment and recreation throughout Britain during the industrial revolution, as rural populations moved to cities. And the British, in turn, spread the game around the world, as skilled workers such as merchants, engineers, and railway builders were in demand to help industrialize other countries. The game quickly caught on, mainly because it was a very simple game and the rules were easy to learn.

At the turn of the 20th century a number of European countries, recognizing the growth of international soccer, suggested the formation of a controlling body that would ensure that all countries played by the same rules. A

Dutch banker, C. A. W. Hirschman, approached the English FA in 1902 to see if it would be interested in helping to organize an international tournament. Though it had previously been such an innovative organization, the English FA's attitude was surprisingly negative; it repeatedly said it would discuss the subject at the next meeting. After being continually rebuffed, representatives from France, Belgium, Holland, Denmark, Sweden, Switzerland, and Spain held a meeting in Paris on May 21, 1904. It was at this momentous meeting that the *Federation Internationale de Football Association* (FIFA) was founded.

Regretting that they had not taken an active interest from the start, the FA joined FIFA in 1906, only to pull out in 1918, refusing to play "enemy" countries.

At first, FIFA's responsibilities were limited. It did not, and still does not, control the laws of the game, which is technically under the auspices of the International Football Association Board.

But as FIFA's membership has grown, so have its responsibilities. It started by initiating the Olympic Games, soccer tournament and is now a worldwide body with wide-ranging powers.

By World War II over 50 countries were members, and after the war, as more and more countries achieved independence, membership rose further. Thanks to FIFA, continental soccer confederations have been set up around the globe; this has helped raise the profile of the less-established countries of the world. FIFA has a policy to be politically neutral and has expelled countries that have caused political unease. South Africa contravened FIFA's anti-discrimination code and was expelled in the early seventies but was readmitted in 1992.

However, for all its work, FIFA is best known for the

World Cup tournament, the idea for which was considered as early as 1904. In most countries, soccer was played by amateurs and there were therefore no problems of eligibility for the Olympic tournament. The winners were, quite rightly, regarded as the world champions. However, in the 1920s, some of the major powers in soccer, notably Czechoslovakia, Austria, and Hungary, introduced professionalism to their national game and were unable to send their strongest teams to the Olympic competition. There were also doubts concerning the amateur status of some of the South American teams, all of which served to reduce the credibility of the Olympic tournament.

At FIFA's congress in Amsterdam in 1928 a motion was proposed by Jules Rimet, FIFA's president, that another world tournament should be held, also every four years, and open to any FIFA member. The motion was passed 25 votes to 5, and the Jules Rimet Trophy was commissioned.

The honor of hosting the inaugural tournament fell to Uruguay—they were the current Olympic champions, it was the the centenary of their independence, and they offered to pay all the visiting teams' travel and accommodations. Besides, the other bidding countries systematically withdrew as they realized how much of a financial burden they would have to take on.

RULES:
HOW IT'S PLAYED

The laws of soccer are not etched in stone. Like most modern team sports, soccer is constantly evolving, and its rules have been subject to frequent amendment since they were first drawn up in London in 1863.

Among the new rules for USA '94, for example, is that now three points rather than two will be awarded for a win in the group stage matches. This change was brought in as a reaction to the negative approach of many teams at the 1990 World Cup, and is designed to reward teams that adopt an attacking approach.

Some parts of the game, however, are regarded as sacrosanct—and not just by the purists. One recent suggestion that the size of the goals should be increased was treated with the sort of scorn that would be heaped on the suggestion that the pitcher's mound in baseball be moved six feet farther away from home plate. Some things are here to stay.

This is not intended as a comprehensive guide to all the laws of soccer. But if it gives those who will be watching the World Cup as soccer novices a basic understanding of most of its rules, and deepens the knowledge of those who are already familiar with the game, it will have served its purpose.

FIELD OF PLAY

FIFA has stipulated that for the World Cup venues, the field must have a minimum length of 115 yards and a minimum width of 75 yards. The Meadowlands in New Jersey is the exception. Because it was built as an American football–only stadium (for a field 53.3 yards wide) the maximum width it can bear—allowing space for throw-ins, dugouts, and corner kicks—is 72 yards, but this has been accepted by FIFA.

Field markings are very basic and easy to follow. You will hear television commentators referring to the penalty box, the goal line, the touchline, the halfway line, and the center circle.

The field is divided in two halves by the halfway line, which has a center circle at its midway point with a radius of 10 yards. At the center of the circle is the center spot, where the ball is placed for the kick-off at the beginning of each half and after a goal has been scored.

The goals are 8 yards across and 8 feet high. In front of each goal, a rectangular area 6 yards deep by 20 yards across is marked on the field; this is the goal area, within which goal kicks must be taken. Beyond this, there is another rectangular marking, 18 yards deep by 44 yards across. This is the penalty area, which contains the penalty spot, 12 yards from the goal. A semicircle (known as the "D") extends in an arc outside the penalty area, 10 yards from the penalty spot.

LENGTH OF PLAY

The duration of the game is 90 minutes, consisting of two periods of 45 minutes with a 15-minute break at halftime after which the teams switch halves of the playing field. However, there is no game clock, and timekeeping is the responsibility of the referee, to compensate for deliberate time-wasting by players or for other stoppages of play such as substitutions and injuries. The resulting "injury time" or "time added on" is added to each half accordingly. Time is always allowed for a penalty kick to be taken after the expiration of normal time at the end of either half.

The time a referee blows for full-time can be a matter of controversy. During the 1978 World Cup, Brazil was playing Sweden in Mar del Plata. With the score even at 1–1, the Brazilians won a corner kick in the final minute. The ball came across the goal mouth, and Zico rose to meet it and headed it into the net. However, as Zico made contact, the Welsh referee, Clive Thomas, blew his whistle for the end of the game, and the goal, to Brazil's fury, was not allowed. Thomas insisted that the 90 minutes were up the moment the corner was taken, but his explanation drew an unsympathetic response from FIFA. The implication is that referees are best advised to blow for time when the ball is in a neutral area of the field.

In the knock-out stages of the World Cup, if the score is tied after 90 minutes, half an hour of extra time will be played consisting of two periods of fifteen minutes. It is not "sudden death" as in American football and if no goals are scored in extra time the contest will be decided on a penalty shoot-out (see PENALTIES).

REFEREES AND LINESMEN

The referee enjoys total authority once the game is under way. His decision is final and there is no right of appeal based on the evidence of TV replays. He is the official time-keeper of the game. Though the laws are clear as to which sanctions should apply for various offenses, the referee can use his discretion to decide, for instance, when a particular foul warrants showing a yellow card to the offender.

Referees are equipped with a whistle to order play to stop. They traditionally dress in an all-black outfit, but for these finals referees will wear a green jersey and the lines-men will wear yellow jerseys. The two linesmen, who stand on opposite touchlines, assist the referee by signaling when the ball has gone out of play over the touchline or over the goal line for a goal kick or corner; when a substitute wishes to enter the field of play; and when a player is offside. The referee is under no obligation to accept the linesman's sig-nal, and may even contradict him if, for instance, the ref-eree was in a better position to judge which team last touched the ball before it went over the touchline for a throw-in. The referee is at liberty to confer with his lines-men before making a ruling on a particular play.

Soccer is a continuous game, and the whole pattern of play can change in a split second. The speed at which the ball can be played often puts the referee in a situation where he has to make an instant decision that he considers to be correct at that exact point of play. Post- mortems on games invariably question the decisions of a referee, but the impe-tus of the game has to be maintained and his word is final.

The 22 referees and 22 linesmen appointed to the World Cup finals underwent a training camp earlier in the year to assess fitness and undergo courses to encour-age a consistent approach in the application of the rules.

PLAYERS

Each team has 11 members, one of whom is a goalkeeper who must wear a shirt that contrasts with those of both teams. Two players from a group of nominated substitutes can be exchanged for an on-field player at any time during the game. Such changes are at the total discretion of the team coach, and might be made because a player suffers an injury, to bring on a fresh pair of legs, or to replace an attacker with a defender to protect a lead late in the game.

Referees are at liberty to order a player to remove any item that they believe poses a danger to other players, be it sharp studs on a player's boots, jewelry, or other items. The start of the 1978 World Cup final was delayed because the Argentinians objected to the Dutchman Rene van der Kerkhof's plaster cast on his arm. The referee ordered him to return to the dressing room to have it padded.

Except when throwing in, a player is not allowed to play the ball with his hands or arms. All players are permitted to use any other part of the body in order to stop, control, or move the ball.

The goalkeeper is unique in being allowed to handle the ball, but only within his own penalty area. If he carries the ball outside his area, a direct free kick is awarded to the opposition. And once he has picked up the ball, he may only take four steps while bouncing or holding the ball before he must release it into play. If he exceeds the four steps, the opposition gains an indirect free kick at the site of the offense.

With the advent of the back-pass rule two years ago to prevent time-wasting, the goalkeeper's lot has become much more difficult. The rule forbids the goalkeeper from handling a ball deliberately played back to him with a teammate's feet (he may pick up a ball headed or chested back to him). This forces the goalkeeper to punt a back pass straight back downfield, or risk a costly error by dribbling around an onrushing forward and passing to a teammate. While some goalkeepers have welcomed the opportunity to display their hitherto unrecognized ball skills, others have seen their miskicked clearance pass punished by a goal.

In the last 30 years, soccer's outfield positions have undergone a tactical revolution. Where once teams would line up rigidly with two fullbacks, three halfbacks, and five forwards, now there is an increased fluidity between defense, midfield, and attack. A typical formation might be four defenders, four midfielders, and two attackers (known as 4-4-2), although there are many variations and strategies, and all systems have had their adherents.

The Italians introduced the sweeper, who plays behind the defense and is responsible for picking up a lone attacker who gets free from defenders. Franz Beckenbauer, who coached West Germany to a 1990 World Cup victory, transformed what is essentially a defensive ploy into an attacking option by developing the role of *libero* (literally "free man"). When his side was defending, Beckenbauer would play as a sweeper, but once it regained possession he would regularly make sorties upfield to provide an extra man in attack, scoring many goals for West Germany during his career.

This move to greater flexibility in player positions accelerated in the 1970s, with the Dutch leading the way with their concept of "total football," which basically meant that any player should be comfortable with positions other than his own. Defenders were expected to be just as adept in attack. They had to be able to pass their way out of trouble rather than rely on the traditional punt upfield. Forwards were expected to drop back and help in defense.

Under the traditional soccer lineup, the center forward was the star of the team. Wearing the number 9 shirt meant that he was the main goal-scorer and was expected to complete the moves. Nowadays, midfield playmakers like Roberto Baggio of Italy are the game's real stars. Rather like the quarterback in American football, they make the bullets for others to fire. They must search for an opening amid the packed defense of the modern game, splitting the defense with a through ball, taking on and beating opponents with skillful close control, or shooting for goal themselves.

SUMMARY OF POSITIONS

Goalkeeper: Must have good handling to catch the ball or punch it clear of danger. He must be very agile to cover all corners of the goal. He must also be quick to race out and beat an opponent to the ball, smother a shot, or reduce the opponent's options and angles to the goal. This requires courage to throw one's body and block a shot, often when several players are racing for the ball. There is always a danger of getting hurt.

A goalkeeper also has the best vision of the whole field, and he will be shouting instructions, particularly to his defenders, to organize the defense. Even though the goalkeeper is the last line of defense, he must also be aware enough to see the opportunities of starting a quick counterattack.

Defenders: A defender's main objective is to prevent an opponent's attack either by getting to the ball first, tackling an opponent, or making it difficult to shoot at the goal or pass to a teammate. However, a defender must also be able to start his team's offensive options and provide support in attacking situations.

The fullbacks will support the attack by making runs down the right and left flanks and producing crosses into the center of the goal area. The central defenders are often seen in the penalty area for corners and free kicks, where they will use their height and heading power to score.

Midfielders: Midfielders have developed into the true stars of the game. They are responsible for creating attacking opportunities as well as assisting in the defense with timely interceptions and tackles. This role requires a lot of stamina as the player has to cover a lot of ground. One moment he might be winning the ball in defense; the next he will be supplying accurate passes to his strikers and making himself available for a return pass from which he might score. Players like Lothar Matthaus (Germany) and David Platt (England) exemplify this role.

There is another style of midfielder, commonly known as the playmaker, whose role it is to create goalscoring chances with a touch of genius. These players possess excellent individual skill and vision and are on the team to breach an opponent's defense with an accurate pass or by beating defenders themselves. They will be the most tightly marked men in the competition but players with the skill of Roberto Baggio (Italy), Carlos Valderrama (Colombia), and Gheorge Hagi (Romania) are exciting to watch as they are always likely to try something creative.

A striker's sole role is to score goals. Some may help out in midfield when the team is under pressure but a striker must take his chances in front of the goal. They may not always score the most spectacular goals but a good striker has the knack of being in the right place at the right time. To watch some of the great players like Brazil's Romario and Dutch star Dennis Bergkamp, it appears to be almost instinctive the way they time their runs into the penalty area to meet a cross or pass, getting to the ball before an opponent to direct a shot or header past the goalkeeper. They are often quick over short distances, quick to turn, quick to spot a loose ball, and quick to pounce.

The Golden Boot Award is presented to me top goal-scorer in the tournament, won, in recent times, by Italy's Toto Schillaci, and England's Gary Lineker.

YELLOW AND RED CARDS

When the referee shows a yellow card to a player, this is known as a caution or booking; when he shows a red card, this is a sending-off, and the player may take no fur-ther part in the game. Once a player has been cautioned, if he commits another offense warranting a yellow card, the referee will show first a yellow and then a red card, indicating that the player has been sent off for two cau-tionable offenses.

The showing of yellow or red cards by a referee also results in the awarding of a free kick. There are a number of offenses that are laid down as sending-off offenses:

- violent conduct
- serious foul play
- foul and abusive language
- bringing down an attacker deliberately when he has a clear goal-scoring chance

Obviously these depend on the interpretation of the referee, as do the grounds for showing a player a yellow card. A yellow card may be shown for:

- a deliberate foul when there is no direct chance of scoring

- refusing to follow the referee's instruction to move back 10 yards at a free kick
- tangling with an opponent after a hard tackle

The referee's judgment is naturally going to be colored by the context of the game; if discipline is breaking down, the next foul is likely to result in a booking. But if the offense is seen as an aberration in a generally clean game, the offender may get off with a strong word from the referee. The laws cannot legislate for every eventuality, but before the World Cup all the referees will be given specific instructions designed to achieve consistency throughout the tournament.

In past World Cups a player acquiring two yellow cards (in different games) was suspended for one game. This year each player's yellow-card slate will be wiped clean after the first-round games. This does not apply to red cards. There is a risk that this will encourage, not deter, cynical fouls in group matches.

KICK-OFFS, THROW-INS, GOAL KICKS, CORNER KICKS

All of these are ways of starting or restarting the game when the ball has gone out of play.

At the start of the game, the two captains toss a coin, with the winner choosing either to kick off, or to select which end his team will play toward in the first half. The kick-off is taken from the center spot, and the opposing team must retreat 10 yards outside the center circle. After a goal is scored, the team that has conceded the goal kicks off in the same way.

When the ball goes over the touchline, a throw-in is awarded to the opponents of the player who last touched it, at the point at which it crossed the line. This throw is taken two-handed from above the head, with both feet touching the ground on release. Some players can reach the goal area with a throw-in, and this is often an effective attacking option. This ruling is currently under review and may be replaced by a kick-in. However, it is a healthy sign that even traditional acts of play are open to improvement.

When the ball crosses the goal line on either side of or above the goal, a goal kick is awarded if a player of the attacking team was the last to touch it, while a corner kick is given if the ball was last touched by the defending team. Goal kicks, generally taken by the goalkeeper, must be taken from inside the goal area, and to the side of the goal where the ball went out of play.

Corner kicks are taken by the attacking team from the quarter-circle in the corner of the field where the ball went out of play. Defenders must retreat 10 yards at a corner kick, so attackers may either loft the ball into the goalmouth or play it short to a teammate to seek out a better angle for a cross.

FREE KICKS

Offenses generally result in the opposition being awarded two kinds of free kicks—direct or indirect—except for offenses in the penalty area, which may result in a penalty kick (see PENALTIES). Offenses that result in a direct free kick, from which a goal may be scored directly, include:

- tripping an opponent
- holding an opponent
- playing the ball with a hand or arm
- kicking an opponent
- jumping at an opponent

- striking or attempting to strike an opponent
- charging in a violent or dangerous manner

Shoulder charges, however, made shoulder-to-shoulder against a player in possession of the ball and with the intention of separating him from it, are permitted.

Offenses resulting in an indirect free kick include:

- time-wasting
- obstruction
- goalkeeper taking more than four steps holding the ball
- dangerous play
- offside

A player cannot score from an indirect free kick unless another player touches the ball before it enters the goal. The defending team must always retreat 10 yards until a free kick is taken. If the free kick is within goal-scoring range, you will often see a team forming a human wall to reduce the chance of the opposition scoring. They will also try to block a shot by charging at the ball but they must remain 10 yards from the ball until it is kicked.

PENALTIES

Penalties are awarded to the attacking team when an offense that would result in a direct free kick is committed by a player inside his own penalty area. When a penalty is being taken, the goalkeeper must not move until the kick is taken, although this is a difficult matter to judge. All the other players must be at least 10 yards from the penalty spot, outside the area and beyond the D. Players other than the penalty-taker may only enter the area once the kick has been taken. The penalty-taker may not play the ball again once the kick is taken until it has touched another player. If, for instance, his kick is parried by the goalkeeper, he may follow up and score from the rebound, but not if it rebounds from a post. Another player from his team, however, may score from a rebound off a post if he can get to it more quickly than the defending team.

Rules governing penalties are slightly different in the penalty shoot-out. Here, a penalty only counts if it enters the goal direct from the spot. If the goalkeeper prevents the ball from entering the goal, the penalty-taker may not follow up to score.

OFFSIDE

This is the most contentious rule in soccer. The offside rule is a tactical law designed to prevent attacking players from waiting near their opponents' goal for the ball. Simply stated, the rule is that a player in his opponents' half and nearer to his opponents' goal line than the ball will be ruled offside if, at the moment the ball is played by a teammate, he has fewer than two opponents (one of whom may be the goalkeeper) nearer their own goal line than he is. There are exceptions to the rule. A player cannot be offside direct from a throw-in, a goal kick, or a corner kick. Neither is a player offside—and here is where the arguments start—if the referee decides that he is not interfering with play or with an opponent, nor seeking to gain an advantage by being in an offside position. One famous English manager of the 1960s said of the latter rule that if one of his players was not interfering with play, then what was he doing on the field?

Many linesmen tend to ignore the point about interfering with play and simply raise their flag to signal offside as soon as any attacking player strays behind the last defender when the ball is played. There will be no shortage of offside rulings to argue about during the USA World Cup.

It is a part of some teams' strategy to force the offside by continually moving defenders up the field, therefore breaking the flow of the opposing team, who have to ensure their players are not occupying an offside position.

When a player is ruled offside, the opposing team gains an indirect free kick from the place where the offense occurred.

GOALS

Finally we come to the rules covering the scoring of goals, which is, of course, the purpose of the game. A goal is awarded if the whole of the ball is deemed to have crossed the goal line between the posts and under the crossbar. Since referees are rarely directly in line to rule on situations where, say, a defender hooks the ball out from under his crossbar when it is traveling over the line, linesmen often become the final court of appeal.

The most famous instance of this occurred during extra time in the 1966 World Cup final between West Germany and England. The English striker turned and fired a shot toward the German goal. The ball hit the underside of the crossbar, bounced straight down, and spun away from the goal. The English players appealed that it was a goal, while the Germans insisted that it had not crossed the line. The referee consulted with his linesman and after a quick discussion signaled a goal, putting England ahead 3–2. Evidence suggests that all of the ball did not cross the line, but fortunately Geoff Hurst scored a fourth goal for England to put matters beyond reach.

THE WORLD CUP
COMPETITION HISTORY

 URUGUAY 1930

While European football was being thrown into disarray by the effects of the First World War, the game was being enjoyed in North America and fanatically in South America. In 1913, the United States Football Association was born and joined the world governing body, FIFA, the same year. Three years later, the *Federacion Sudamericana de Football* was set up, a year that also saw Uruguay become the inaugural winner of the South American Championship which included Argentina, Brazil, and Chile.

The only true international soccer event at this time was the Olympic tournament. At the Paris Olympics in 1924, Uruguay took the title with a team that included professional players. Uruguay retained their title at the 1928 Amsterdam Olympics, but fielded professional players once again.

If there was to be a true world championship of football, where the best players would meet, then it would have to be independent of the Olympics, so in 1928 FIFA made the decision to host the first World Cup.

Uruguay, Holland, Hungary, Italy, Spain, and Sweden put their names forward as potential hosts but one by one they all pulled out until it was left to Uruguay.

Thirteen countries made the trip to Montevideo in Uruguay. Europe sent only four teams: Romania, France, Belgium, and Yugoslavia. Surprisingly, none of the other countries who had put their names forward as hosts decided to enter.

Romania was not supposed to be sending a team but the young King Carol, a keen soccer fan, requested employers to give three months' leave to any employees picked for the team. They agreed, and King Carol selected the team himself.

France, although they knew that their team was not up to the standard of the South Americans, felt obliged to send a team, since they had been instrumental in getting the World Cup tournament off the ground. Some wondered why Belgium and Yugoslavia even bothered to make the long trip.

The tournament was a success and packed with drama. In the opening game, France beat Mexico, and the honor of scoring the first World Cup goal fell to Frenchman Lucien Laurent. The French won 4–1, but not before their goalkeeper had been kicked in the head and was unable to continue. (Until 1970 and a revision in the rules, substitutions were not allowed.) In their second match, against Argentina, the French were one goal down but outplaying the opposition and looking certain to score an equalizing goal when the Brazilian referee blew for full time, ending the match six minutes early. The spectators invaded the field and France protested. The remaining time was eventually played, but France never got back into the game.

Controversy followed Argentina everywhere. In their

6–3 win over Mexico the referee awarded five penalties, and their game against Chile turned into a brawl after a foul by the Argentine, Luisito Monti. The police were called in to separate the players.

The United States was the surprise team of the competition. They had been beaten 11–2 by Argentina in the 1928 Olympics but since then many British professionals had emigrated to the States and were now members of the national team. They were probably past their best in footballing terms—some of them were rather big and heavy, a detail the French were quick to pick up on, nicknaming them the shot-putters. Despite this, their team had considerable stamina and enthusiasm, beating Belgium and Paraguay before succumbing to Argentina in a tough semifinal. The United States's center half, Raphael Tracy, had his leg broken after only 10 minutes, and their goalkeeper suffered numerous injuries. Argentina was not to be stopped and took the match 6–1.

Uruguay had also won their semifinal, 6–1, so the final became a rerun of the 1928 Olympic final. Relations were strained between the host nation and Argentina. It didn't help when Argentine supporters, who arrived in boats from across the Plata River, were searched for weapons at the docks and before entering the grounds. In a close match, the Argentinians had the better of the first half, leading 2–1 at the interval. But with the majority of the 93,000 in the crowd cheering for the home side, Uruguay breached the Argentine defense three times to take the title, 4–2—the final goal being scored in the closing minute by Castro, the center forward who had the lower half of one arm missing.

Montevideo erupted into celebration—their team's win was the crowning glory in such a significant year in their country's history.

GROUP ONE

France	4	Mexico	1
Argentina	1	France	0
Chile	3	Mexico	0
Chile	1	France	0
Argentina	6	Mexico	3
Argentina	3	Chile	1

FINAL TABLE

	Played	Won	Drawn	Lost	Goals For	Goals Against	Pts.
Argentina	3	3	0	0	10	4	6
Chile	3	2	0	1	5	3	4
France	3	1	0	2	4	3	2
Mexico	3	0	0	3	4	13	0

GROUP TWO

Yugoslavia	2	Brazil	1
Yugoslavia	4	Bolivia	0
Brazil	4	Bolivia	0

FINAL TABLE

	Played	Won	Drawn	Lost	Goals For	Goals Against	Pts.
Yugoslavia	2	2	0	0	6	1	4
Brazil	2	1	0	1	5	2	2
Bolivia	2	0	0	2	0	8	0

GROUP THREE

Romania	3	Peru	1
Uruguay	1	Peru	0
Uruguay	4	Romania	0

FINAL TABLE

	Played	Won	Drawn	Lost	Goals For	Goals Against	Pts.
Uruguay	2	2	0	0	5	0	4
Romania	2	1	0	1	3	5	2
Peru	2	0	0	2	1	4	0

GROUP FOUR

United States	3	Belgium	0
United States	3	Paraguay	0
Paraguay	1	Belgium	0

FINAL TABLE

	Played	Won	Drawn	Lost	Goals For	Goals Against	Pts.
United States	2	2	0	0	6	0	4
Paraguay	2	1	0	1	1	3	2
Belgium	2	0	0	2	0	4	0

SEMIFINALS

Argentina	6	United States	1
Uruguay	6	Yugoslavia	1

FINAL

Uruguay	4	Argentina	2

Top goal-scorers: 8 Stabile (Argentina); 5 Cea (Uruguay); 4 Subiabre (Chile); 3 Anselmo (Uruguay); 3 Beck (Yugoslavia); 3 Patenaude (United States); 3 Peucelle (Argentina); 3 Preguinho (Brazil).

Fastest goal: 1 minute, Desu (Romania vs. Peru).

Most goals scored: 18 Argentina.

Total goals scored: 70 (average 3.88 per game).

Total attendance: 434,500 (average 24,139 per game).

Final attendance: 93,000.

ITALY 1934

It took eight lengthy meetings by FIFA to confirm Italy as the host venue for the 1934 tournament. It was a strange choice of venue, as Italy was under the dictatorial control of Mussolini, who viewed the competition as a great propaganda opportunity, although government backing ensured that it would be a well-funded and well-organized event.

For the first and only time in the history of the competition the holders of the trophy did not defend their title. Uruguay stayed at home, upset that so few European teams had agreed to compete in their tournament four years earlier.

The second World Cup established the number of finalists at 16, which was considered sufficient until 1982. Because the number of actual entrants was 32, qualifying rounds were needed to reduce the number of teams to 16 for the final tournament which was to be played on a purely knock-out basis. Even the host nation, Italy, had to qualify, which they did comfortably. They were installed as one of the eight seeded nations—a system devised to avoid pairing the strongest nations together in the first round.

The United States was a late entrant and missed the qualifying round, but FIFA decided that the United States should play Mexico, the winner of qualifying Group One, in Rome. Hence both teams had to make the long trip fully aware that they might be eliminated after only one game. This unhappy fate fell to Mexico.

On May 27, 1934, in the magnificent Rome Stadium, Italy got the competition under way with an impressive 7–1 victory over the United States.

After dominating the first World Cup, the South American contingent failed to get past the first round this time. Brazil lost to Spain while Argentina, which had lost many of their finest players to the Italian League and had decided to keep their star players at home, now fielded a weak team that couldn't match the industry of the Swedes.

Egypt became the first African nation to compete in the World Cup and was far from disgraced in defeat to Hungary, one of Europe's strongest teams.

Of the remaining teams, Germany was uninspiring in their victory over Belgium; Czechoslovakia struggled against Romania; and even the Austrians, nicknamed the "Wunderteam" and one of the favorites, were fortunate in beating the French.

On to the second round, where Italy was drawn to play Spain. In a bruising encounter Regueiro put the Spanish into the lead, but shortly after halftime Ferrari equalized for Italy, much to the delight and relief of the home supporters. The score remained level after extra time and both teams had to make dramatic changes as a result of injuries for the replay the following day. Despite fielding a depleted team, Spain did well to limit Italy to one goal, scored by Meazza in the 12th minute, and were unlucky to have two goals disallowed in controversial circumstances.

Austria defeated Hungary in a game that Austrian manager Hugo Meisl described as "a brawl, not a football match," which set up a semifinal against Italy—a match many people had hoped would be the final. Italy was thankful for Guaita, one of their three Argentinian players, when he scored the decisive goal in the first half. The Italian manager, Vittorio Pozzo, had molded a great side, but he still felt the need to field the three Argentinians, who were of Italian extraction. He did point out that all three had Italian fathers and said, "If they can die for Italy, they can play football for Italy."

Austria failed to have a shot on target for most of the first half but applied sustained pressure after the interval, only to be thwarted by the Italian goalkeeper Combi. The home crowd, which included Mussolini, was delighted.

For the other semifinal, in front of only 10,000 spectators, Czechoslovakia, with three goals from Nejedly, outplayed a well-organized but uninspired German side to book their place in the final. Three days before the final Germany beat an obviously tired Austrian team in the third-place play-off—a match that has always been a dubious fixture, a feeling which the Italian public shared, as only 7,000 turned out to watch.

And so on to an intriguing final. The Italians had proved they were a strong, powerful team, but the stylish Czechs were looking capable of producing an upset. Despite both sides showing a positive approach to the game, it was 70 minutes before the Czechs took the lead through Puc, who had only just returned to the field after suffering from cramp. Czechoslovakia had two more golden opportunites to make the game safe, but with only eight minutes remaining Italy scored a spectacular equalizer. Orsi received the ball from his fellow Argentinian, Guaita, ran through the Czech defense, and struck the ball, which swerved past the goalkeeper's desperate dive and into the net, taking the final into extra time. The next day, Orsi tried to repeat the shot for photographers but failed.

The teams had been evenly matched, but the stamina of the Italians now held them in good stead. The Czech defense neglected to mark Meazza, who was limping through injury, but he played a telling ball to Guaita who, in turn, found Schiavio. With a final effort Schiavio beat a defender and then the goalkeeper for what proved to be the winning goal.

Italy was the world champion and their captain, goal-keeper Combi, received the trophy from Mussolini, who hailed it as a victory for Fascism. Even though the tournament had been used as a political tool, the number of participants and interest in the competition had been considerable and the Italian team had simply set new standards of teamwork and professionalism.

FIRST ROUND

Italy	7	United States	1
Czechoslovakia	2	Romania	1
Germany	5	Belgium	2
Austria	3	France	2
Spain	3	Brazil	1
Switzerland	3	Holland	2
Sweden	3	Argentina	2
Hungary	4	Egypt	2

SECOND ROUND

Germany	2	Sweden	1
Austria	2	Hungary	1
Italy	1	Spain	1
Italy	1	Spain	0 (replay)
Czechoslovakia	3	Switzerland	2

SEMIFINALS

Italy	1	Austria	0
Czechoslovakia	3	Germany	1

THIRD-PLACE PLAY-OFF

Germany   3   Austria   2

FINAL

Italy   2   Czechoslovakia 1
                  (after extra time)

Top goal-scorers: 5 Nejedly (Czechoslovakia); 4 Conen
  (Germany); 4 Schiavio (Italy); 3 Kielholz (Switzerland);
  3 Orsi (Italy).
Fastest goal: 30 seconds, Lehner (Germany vs. Austria)
Most goals scored: 12 Italy.
Total goals scored: 70 (average 4.12 per game).
Total attendance: 395,000 (average 23,235 per game).
Final attendance: 55,000.

FRANCE 1938

Only two years after Hitler had used the Berlin Olympics as a political statement and with Europe in turmoil and on the brink of war, FIFA was left with a difficult choice of host country for the third World Cup.

The decision went to France, a popular choice, as it was the home country of Jules Rimet, whose dream it had been to stage a World Cup tournament. As a result, Argentina refused to take part, upset at not being selected as hosts—a decision completely against the wishes of their soccer-mad public who rioted in Buenos Aires. It would be another 20 years before they entered a team.

Spain was forced to withdraw on account of their civil war and the Austrians, their country having been taken over by the Nazis in the *Anschluss*, found themselves unable to compete. Germany took advantage by recruiting some of Austria's best players. Only three non-European teams entered—Brazil, Cuba, and the Dutch East Indies —and despite pleas by FIFA, the four British teams still would not enter.

This was the first tournament in which both holders and hosts were exempt from the qualifying competition but, as in 1934, the finals were played as a straight knock-out competition.

In the opening round of matches Switzerland refused to give the Nazi salute during the national anthem and defeated Germany in a replay, while Cuba, making their first and, to date, only World Cup appearance, shocked the Romanians 2–1, also in a replay.

Czechoslovakia, with some of the same players who had finished runners-up to Italy in 1934, were one of the fancied teams but made heavy weather of beating Holland—it was not until extra time that they exerted their superiority. Even the world and Olympic champions, Italy, found their opening game against Norway tough going. An early goal by Ferrari for Italy was canceled out by Brustad's 83d minute equalizer for Norway. The game went into extra time and Italy was relieved to see Piola snatch the winner.

France, the home nation, safely negotiated Belgium, and the strong Hungarian team, which had beaten Greece 11–1 in the qualifying tournament, netted 6 against the Dutch East Indies.

However, the most remarkable match of the tournament was the game between Brazil, the sole South American team, and Poland. In a pulsating match, Brazil took control in the first half to lead 3–1, with Leonidas scoring all three of Brazil's goals. After the interval, Poland hit back to level the score at 3–3; Brazil regained the lead, but with only two minutes remaining Willimowski completed his hat trick for Poland to make the score 4–4. In extra time, Leonidas scored his fourth and Romeo extended Brazil's lead to 6–4. Willimowski also scored his fourth, but it was too late, and Brazil went into the second round.

After such an entertaining and good-natured game, it was sad that Brazil's next match, against Czechoslovakia, should turn into such a disgraceful and bad-tempered affair. Three players were sent off and two Czech players suffered broken limbs. Leonidas—who else—scored for Brazil but Nejedly equalized from the penalty spot. Despite losing Nejedly with a broken leg and with goalkeeper Planicka playing with a broken arm, the Czechs held out to force a replay.

Both teams made sweeping changes for the replay,

which was as docile as the first was violent. Leonidas equalized for Brazil after Kopecky had given the Czechs the lead, and Roberto volleyed the South Americans' winner only one minute from time.

Italy met their French hosts in Paris and although the teams were well-matched, France having held the world champions to a goalless draw only seven months before, it was Italy's goal-scoring sensation Piola who took control in the second half, scoring two goals. The Swedes annihilated Cuba and Hungary eased past Switzerland and into the semifinals.

Brazil's Leonidas and Italy's Piola, two of the game's most prolific goal-scorers, were set to meet in the semifinal but, in a curious decision, Brazil's coach, Pimenta, left Leonidas out of the game, claiming he was saving him for the final. This self-assurance proved to be Brazil's undoing, as first Colaussi and then Meazza, from the penalty spot, scored for Italy. Peracio, the replacement for Leonidas, missed two chances for Brazil, and Romeo's 87th-minute goal came too late for the South Americans.

Hungary had looked an impressive team from the start of the tournament and Sweden was hoping that the fact that the game was being played on the 80th birthday of their monarch King Gustav V might prove a lucky omen.

Sweden did indeed score within the first minute, but this did nothing to deter the Hungarians, who had full control of the game by halftime. Zsengeller completed his hat trick in the 5–1 victory, and so dominant was Hungary that a bird sat undisturbed on the field near their goal for much of the second half.

In the third-place play-off, Sweden again took an unexpected lead, this time against Brazil, who had recalled Leonidas to the team. They went two goals ahead before Romeo pulled one back for Brazil just before halftime. In the second half, Leonidas burst into life, scoring two goals in a 4–2 final score that made many people wonder whether the result against Italy might have been reversed if Leonidas, the tournament's top scorer, had been on the field.

So, Italy had reached their second successive final and the crowd was eager to see how they would cope against the Hungarians, who had scored 13 goals in only three matches with a classic passing game.

The crowd did not have to wait long. Only six minutes into the game Colaussi scored for the Italians following a fantastic run by Biavati, only for Titkos to equalize minutes later. Piola restored Italy's lead and Colaussi extended it before halftime. With 20 minutes remaining, Sarosi reduced the deficit to just one goal, but eight minutes from time Piola, appropriately, scored a fourth for Italy as Hungary was forced into attack.

No one could deny that Italy was a worthy winner. Their manager, Vittorio Pozzo, had thus disproved those skeptics who had suggested Italy could only have won on home soil. To take two different World Cup teams to victory was a great achievement.

The Second World War started just over 12 months later, and it would be 12 long years before the next tournament would take place.

WORLD CUP MEMORY

● ● ● ● ● ● ● ● ● ● ● ● ● ● ● ● ● ● ● ●

Aldo Olivieri, Italian goalkeeper:
"The favorites that year were Italy, Brazil, Hungary and Germany. Germany was very strong, as the country had joined up with Austria and they had five or six Austria play-

ers on the team, but they were knocked out, surprisingly, by Switzerland.

After the World Cup, we were received by the *Duce* [Mussolini] in the Palazzo Venezia in Rome. He gave us all medals, not gold in those days, but bronze. He used to follow football and went to all the games."

● ● ● ● ● ● ● ● ● ● ● ● ● ● ● ● ● ● ●

ROUND ONE

Germany	1	Switzerland	1	
Switzerland	4	Germany	2	(replay)
Cuba	3	Romania	3	
Cuba	2	Romania	1	(replay)
Czechoslovakia	3	Holland	0	
France	3	Belgium	1	
Hungary	6	Dutch East Indies	0	
Italy	2	Norway	1	
Brazil	6	Poland	5	

ROUND TWO

Italy	3	France	1	
Sweden	8	Cuba	0	
Hungary	2	Switzerland	0	
Brazil	1	Czechoslovakia	1	
Brazil	2	Czechoslovakia	1	(replay)

SEMIFINALS

Italy	2	Brazil	1
Hungary	5	Sweden	1

THIRD-PLACE PLAY-OFF

Brazil   4   Sweden   2

FINAL

Italy   4   Hungary   2

Top goal-scorers: 8 Leonidas (Brazil); 7 Zsengeller (Hungary); 5 Piola (Italy); 4 Colaussi (Italy); 4 Sarosi (Hungary); 4 Wetterstrom (Sweden); 4 Willimowski (Poland).

Fastest goal: 35 seconds, Nyberg (Sweden vs. Hungary).

Most goals scored: 15 Hungary.

Total goals scored: 84 (average 4.67 per game).

Total attendance: 483,000 (average 26,833 per game).

Final attendance: 55,000.

BRAZIL 1950

With Europe still in disarray after the war, FIFA took the decision to stage the fourth World Cup tournament in South America. The choice of Brazil, with its fanatical support and enthusiasm for soccer, was a popular one.

However, the qualification for the finals proved farcical and was plagued by withdrawals. From a total of 73 FIFA members, 31 teams, plus Cup holders Italy and hosts Brazil entered the tournament.

The British associations had returned to FIFA in 1946, and the World Cup Committee generously designated the British Championship a qualifying group for two teams. However, although Scotland was guaranteed a place, as they had come second in the group, they decided that as they had not finished top they would not enter.

There were other surprising absentees. Argentina withdrew because of "differences" with the Brazilian FA; Germany was excluded from FIFA as a result of the war; and Austria felt their team was not yet strong enough. Ecuador, Peru, and Belgium also withdrew.

The decision was made to play the tournament in pools rather than the previous system of straight knockout. Each group winner then went through to a final pool, also played on a league basis.

The 15 qualifying teams were divided into four groups, but India subsequently pulled out and France felt that the journey was too long and arduous and also decided not to go. It was too late for FIFA to make another draw, so the tournament got under way with uneven groups. This left Uruguay with only Bolivia in their group, although it seems extraordinary now that a team from one of the two pools with four teams could not have been moved into their pool.

For some obscure reason, the pool matches were not played at a single venue and some teams were obliged to travel huge distances to play their games. Brazil, however, played all but one of their games in Rio.

The competition got under way at the unfinished but impressive Maracana Stadium. Brazil took to the field, welcomed by a 21-gun salute, and an ecstatic crowd saw them beat Mexico, 4–0, with two goals by the brilliant Ademir. However, a nervous draw against the Swiss meant that Brazil had to beat Yugoslavia to progress to the final stage, and although Ademir scored early on, it was not until just after an hour that Zizinho scored Brazil's second—much to the relief of a fanatical crowd of 142,000.

The second pool provided one of the biggest surprises in World Cup history. Both Spain and England had started with victories and the fancied English side now traveled to face the United States, which admittedly had been only ten minutes away from beating Spain. However, no one could have predicted what was to happen. England spent most of the first half attacking, but excellent goalkeeping by Borghi and the resilience of the defense kept England at bay—despite hitting the post and crossbar they could not find the net. But it just seemed a matter of time.

Then eight minutes from halftime, Joe Gaetjens—an American Haitian who was later to disappear, presumed murdered, in Haiti—scored the only goal of the game with a header to bring about the biggest upset in World Cup history. England continued the onslaught but failed to convert any of their chances. It was such an unlikely result that some British newspapers assumed a mistake had been made and printed the score as 10–1. For America, it was their greatest result—particularly as this time their team was composed primarily of American-born players.

England had to beat Spain and gave a much improved performance. England's Milburn had what appeared a good goal disallowed for offside, but it was the Spanish who snatched a 49th-minute winner to take them through to the final pool.

The champions, Italy, competed even though they had suffered a tragic blow when an airplane carrying the brilliant Torino team crashed into the wall of the Superga Basilica on a hillside near Turin in 1949. Every player was killed, including eight of the national team.

The Italian team traveled by boat to Brazil, and although the long journey must have had a detrimental effect on the players, everything appeared to be going well when they opened the scoring against a strong Swedish side. However, three goals stunned the Italians, and although they pulled the score back to 3–2, the equalizer remained elusive. It was their first World Cup defeat. Sweden tied with Paraguay and although Italy beat Paraguay 2–0, it was to no avail. Sweden was through to join Spain, Brazil, and Uruguay, who had beaten Bolivia, 8–0.

Brazil beat the Swedes 7–1 in their first final-pool game, and inflicted six more goals against Spain. They were turning on an exhibition of irresistible footballing skills with the trio of Ademir, Jair, and Zizinho proving themselves players of genius.

While Brazil was in such splendid form, Uruguay, the only team thought to pose a challenge to the hosts, was surprisingly held in a bad-tempered draw against Spain.

Indeed, in their next match against Sweden, Uruguay had to come from a goal down and only scored the winner with five minutes remaining. But they were now the only team capable of taking the Jules Rimet Trophy from Brazil. The scene was set, and although there had been no provision for a final as such, the Brazil versus Uruguay match was to be a final in all but name.

And what a match it turned out to be. A record crowd of nearly 200,000 gathered in the Maracana Stadium to see the game, and everyone was confident of a Brazilian victory—perhaps too confident. Needing only a draw to win the trophy, they relied on attack as the best form of defense, and the first half saw the Brazilians attacking with their now familiar flair. But they were up against a sturdy defense, and for all their superiority of technique the Brazilians were playing a team demonstrating great tactical awareness that was able to soak up the pressure.

Time and again a timely interception or acrobatic save by Maspoli, the Uruguayan goalkeeper, thwarted the Brazilian offense, and the game remained delicately balanced at halftime. Two minutes into the second half the vast crowd erupted as Friaca closed in from the wing, shot, and scored for Brazil. But having survived for so long, Uruguay had made their point and were not demoralized. They responded by attacking, and the talented Schiaffino equalized.

The Brazilians continued to press forward when they could have fallen back into defense, but about 10 minutes from the end the unthinkable happened as Ghiggia put Uruguay ahead with a great individual effort. Uruguay held out until the referee blew the final whistle, signaling the end of an impossible victory. After 20 years, Uruguay was once again world champion.

WORLD CUP MEMORY

● ● ● ● ● ● ● ● ● ● ● ● ● ● ● ● ● ●

Harry Keough, American defender:

"I have a vivid memory of the moment we scored our goal against England. Walter Bahr, our star player, took a shot at the English goal from 25 to 30 yards out. He hit the ball well, but I expected the goalkeeper to stop it. It was then that Joe Gaetjens lunged at the ball and I thought, gee, what's Joe trying to do? He didn't make full contact and he just singed it with his head. Once it touched Joe's head, nobody saw it until it was in the goal.

"We were just a bunch of amateurs playing against a bunch of professionals and nobody on our team had the wildest hope that we would beat England."

● ● ● ● ● ● ● ● ● ● ● ● ● ● ● ● ● ●

GROUP ONE

Brazil	4	Mexico	0
Yugoslavia	3	Switzerland	0
Brazil	2	Switzerland	2
Yugoslavia	4	Mexico	1
Brazil	2	Yugoslavia	0
Switzerland	2	Mexico	1

FINAL TABLE

	Played	Won	Drawn	Lost	Goals For	Goals Against	Pts.
Brazil	3	2	1	0	8	2	5
Yugoslavia	3	2	0	1	7	3	4
Switzerland	3	1	1	1	4	6	3
Mexico	3	0	0	3	2	10	0

GROUP TWO

Spain	3	United States	1
England	2	Chile	0
United States	1	England	0
Spain	2	Chile	0
Spain	1	England	0
Chile	5	United States	2

FINAL TABLE

	Played	Won	Drawn	Lost	Goals For	Goals Against	Pts.
Spain	3	3	0	0	6	1	6
England	3	1	0	2	2	2	2
Chile	3	1	0	2	5	6	2
United States	3	1	0	2	4	8	2

GROUP THREE

Sweden	3	Italy	2
Sweden	2	Paraguay	2
Italy	2	Paraguay	0

FINAL TABLE

	Played	Won	Drawn	Lost	Goals For	Goals Against	Pts.
Sweden	2	1	1	0	5	4	3
Italy	2	1	0	1	4	3	2
Paraguay	2	0	1	1	2	4	1

GROUP FOUR

Uruguay	8	Bolivia	0

FINAL TABLE

	Played	Won	Drawn	Lost	Goals For	Goals Against	Pts.
Uruguay	1	1	0	0	8	0	2
Bolivia	1	0	0	1	0	8	0

FINAL POOL MATCHES

Brazil	7	Sweden	1
Spain	2	Uruguay	2
Brazil	6	Spain	1
Uruguay	3	Sweden	2
Sweden	3	Spain	1
Uruguay	2	Brazil	1

FINAL POSITIONS

	Played	Won	Drawn	Lost	Goals For	Goals Against	Pts.
Uruguay	3	2	1	0	7	5	5
Brazil	3	2	0	1	14	4	4
Sweden	3	1	0	2	6	11	2
Spain	3	0	1	2	4	11	1

Top goal-scorers: 9 Ademir (Brazil); 5 Basora (Spain); 5 Schiaffino (Uruguay); 4 Chico (Brazil); 4 Ghiggia (Uruguay); 4 Miguez, Zarra (Spain); 3 Cremaschi (Chile); 3 Palmer, Sundqvist (Sweden); 3 Tomasevic (Yugoslavia).

Fastest goal: 2 minutes, Santos (Brazil vs. Sweden).

Most goals scored: 22 Brazil.

Total goals scored: 88 (average 4 per game).

Total attendance: 1,337,000 (average 60,772 per game).

Final attendance: 199,854.

SWITZERLAND 1954

The World Cup in Switzerland produced some of the finest attacking football in the tournament's history. It was no surprise that Hungary, the 1952 Olympic champion, was the favorite as for the past few years they had been, quite simply, unbeatable. They were the finest attacking team seen up to then—and possibly even to this day—based on a deep-lying center forward, Nandor Hidegkuti, who controlled much of the build-up and could score goals; a tenacious midfield dynamo, Josef Bozsik; and two great strikers, Ferenc Puskas and Sandor Kocsis.

Such was the skill of the Hungarian team that, in 1953, they became the first team to beat England at Wembley, by a sensational 6–3 margin. England fared no better in the return match in Budapest, losing 7–1.

Football's governing body devised a new eliminating scheme for the finals, reverting to a pool system followed by knock-out. The 16 participants were divided into four groups with two teams in each group seeded, keeping the supposedly stronger teams apart in the early stages. However, the seeded teams in each group did not play each other. At the end of the pool matches, the four group winners were to play each other on a knock-out basis, as were the four runners-up. To complete a complicated system, it was decided that in the pool matches, extra time would be played if the scores were tied after 90 minutes.

West Germany returned, as did the Eastern European bloc with the exception of the Soviet Union and Poland. Argentina was again noticeable by its absence.

In Group One, there was a shock on the opening day

when Yugoslavia beat seeded France 1–0 with a goal from Milos Milutinovic. Although they were somewhat underrated, the Yugoslav team was an impressive blend of youth and experience and their match against Brazil, which was to decide who came top in the group, was a very even game, a 1–1 draw.

In Group Two, the Hungarians served notice by routing South Korea 9–0, and West Germany 8–3. In the second of these games, Sepp Herberger, the West German manager, took a big gamble. He knew that if his team lost to Hungary they would have to play off against either Turkey or South Korea to qualify for the second phase. He also realized that the winner of the group would meet Brazil—a daunting prospect. Confident of beating Turkey or South Korea, he completely changed his team for the game against Hungary.

Despite the onslaught of goals, the plan worked, as Germany, back to full strength, next beat Turkey 7–2 to set up a quarterfinal clash with Yugoslavia. Perhaps the most important aspect of the game was the injury to the Hungarian captain, Puskas, who was to miss the next two games and struggled to regain fitness for the final.

In Group Three, Uruguay, still inspired by Schiaffino, ended Scotland's first World Cup venture with a 7–0 annihilation and qualified to meet England in the quarterfinals. This proved to be a tight and eventful game with Matthews and Wright shining for England, and Schiaffino and Varela outstanding for the South Americans. Both teams created a lot of good scoring chances, but Uruguay's superior all-around qualities coupled with a series of bad errors from the English goalkeeper swung the game in their favor.

The host nation, Switzerland, had made a successful start against Italy in the opening round, but a subsequent defeat by England meant that they had to play Italy again in a decider. A second victory took them through to face Austria and a 12-goal bonanza. Roared on by the home crowd, the Swiss scored three times in the first 20 minutes only for Austria to score five in the next 10 minutes. At halftime the score was 5–4 Austria, who increased their lead to two goals shortly after the restart. Not to be outdone, Switzerland came back again but could find no answer to Austria's seventh. The 12-goal extravaganza established a World Cup record.

Having avoided Brazil, Sepp Herberger's West Germany now faced a useful Yugoslavian team. West Germany took an early lead, withstood everything their opponents could throw at them, and sealed victory with a second goal, against the run of play, shortly before the end.

The fourth quarterfinal between Brazil and Hungary promised to be the game of the tournament, pitching two great football teams against each other. The match, since referred to as the Battle of Berne, witnessed some dreadful tackles and niggling fouls and the only person to emerge with any credit was referee Arthur Ellis, who sent three players off.

Even without Puskas, Hungary started briskly and was two goals up inside the first 10 minutes, seemingly well on their way to the semifinals. But Brazil started to find their form, and a penalty reduced the deficit to 2–1 at halftime. The second half started with more bad fouls and dangerous tackling as tempers frayed. Hungary was awarded a penalty from which Lantos scored, only for Julinho to score a marvelous goal for Brazil. Soon afterward Bozsik and Nilton Santos came to blows after another dangerous challenge and both were sent off.

Brazil was desperately chasing an equalizer and came close to leveling the match several times. However, pushing forward left them exposed in defense and in the last minute Kocsis scored Hungary's fourth to put the result beyond reach. Humberto was also sent off for Brazil, but the fighting continued even after the game had finished, with the teams scuffling in the dressing rooms.

After this disgraceful episode, the semifinal between Hungary and Uruguay turned out to be one of the greatest matches seen—even though both teams were without influential players, Puskas and Varela respectively.

Hungary led 1–0 at the interval and extended their lead early in the second half. Uruguay looked on their way out, but they had never been beaten in a World Cup match, and once again mounted a determined comeback. With 15 minutes to go, Schiffiano put Hohberg through to score and, with only three minutes remaining, they combined again to level the score and force the game into extra time. It nearly began without Hohberg, who had been knocked out during the celebrations by his teammates. He recovered in time to drive a shot against the Hungarian post, but it was not to be a fairy-tale ending for Uruguay. Their midfield inspiration, Andrade, was hurt in a tackle, and while he was still having treatment off the field, Kocsis headed Hungary back into the lead. There was no coming back from that, and Kocsis rose majestically again to score another superb header.

Most people expected Austria to join Hungary in the final but the West Germans were now a very effective team. Austria recalled Walter Zeman—a goalkeeper previously left out because of poor form. Unfortunately for Zeman, it was not a happy return, as he and his defense struggled to combat the West German attack, which swept them into the final with a 6–1 victory.

Even though West Germany had proved themselves a shrewd and worthy finalists, victory was surely a formality for Hungary, particularly once Puskas and Czibor had given them a 2–0 lead by the 8th minute of play. But then the West Germans showed those battling, never-say-die qualities that have since become a World Cup tradition. Morlock and Rahn quickly tied the score and five minutes from the end, Rahn put West Germany in front. A reply by Puskas, who was still struggling from injury, was disallowed, controversially, for offside, and West Germany had pulled off an amazing comeback to become world champions. For the second successive tournament the favorites had been beaten.

GROUP ONE

Yugoslavia	1	France	0
Brazil	5	Mexico	0
France	3	Mexico	2
Brazil	1	Yugoslavia	1

FINAL TABLE

	Played	Won	Drawn	Lost	Goals For	Goals Against	Pts.
Brazil	2	1	1	0	6	1	3
Yugoslavia	2	1	1	0	2	1	3
France	2	1	0	1	3	3	2
Mexico	2	0	0	2	2	8	0

GROUP TWO

Hungary	9	South Korea	0
West Germany	4	Turkey	1
Hungary	8	West Germany	3
Turkey	7	South Korea	0

FINAL TABLE

	Played	Won	Drawn	Lost	Goals For	Goals Against	Pts.
Hungary	2	2	0	0	17	3	4
Turkey	2	1	0	1	8	4	2
West Germany	2	1	0	1	7	9	2
South Korea	2	0	0	2	0	16	0

Play-off: West Germany   7   Turkey   2

GROUP THREE

Austria	1	Scotland	0
Uruguay	2	Czechoslovakia	0
Austria	5	Czechoslovakia	0
Uruguay	7	Scotland	0

FINAL TABLE

	Played	Won	Drawn	Lost	Goals For	Goals Against	Pts.
Uruguay	2	2	0	0	9	0	4
Austria	2	2	0	0	6	0	4
Czechoslovakia	2	0	0	2	0	7	0
Scotland	2	0	0	2	0	8	0

GROUP FOUR

England	4	Belgium	4
Switzerland	2	Italy	1
England	2	Switzerland	0
Italy	4	Belgium	1

FINAL TABLE

	Played	Won	Drawn	Lost	Goals For	Goals Against	Pts.
England	2	1	1	0	6	4	3
Italy	2	1	0	1	5	3	2
Switzerland	2	1	0	1	2	3	2
Belgium	2		0	1	15	8	1

Play-off: Switzerland 4 Italy 1

QUARTERFINALS

Austria	7	Switzerland	5
Uruguay	4	England	2
Hungary	4	Brazil	2
West Germany	2	Yugoslavia	0

SEMIFINALS

Hungary	4	Uruguay	2
West Germany	6	Austria	1

THIRD-PLACE PLAY-OFF

Austria	3	Uruguay	1

FINAL

West Germany   3   Hungary   2

Top goal-scorers: 11 Kocsis (Hungary); 6 Hugi (Switzerland); 6 Morlock (West Germany); 5 Probst (Austria).
Fastest goal: 2 minutes, Suat (Turkey vs. West Germany).
Most goals scored: 27 (Hungary).
Total goals scored: 140 (average 5.38 per game).
Total attendance: 943,000 (average 36,270 per game).
Final attendance: 60,000.

SWEDEN 1958

For the first time in its history, the World Cup received international television coverage. This is remembered as one of the friendliest tournaments, and although a number of players shone, this competition was highlighted by the outstanding skills of the Brazilians and in particular the debut of a 17-year-old genius, Pele. In the Brazilian team, the world witnessed a stunning brand of football that was to become very familiar over the next decade.

The host, Sweden, was coached by an Englishman, George Raynor, who astounded everyone by confidently predicting, long before the tournament began, that his team would reach the final. Few took him seriously, and even the Swedish public displayed little patriotism.

In their opening game, Sweden made light work of the Mexicans, disposing of them, 3–0, before beating the once mighty Hungary 2–1. After a convincing victory over the Soviet Union in the quarterfinals the Swedish fans started to believe in their team. Initially skeptical, this traditionally dispassionate nation reached levels of patriotic euphoria when Sweden beat an unsettled West Germany, the 1954 champions, 3–1. George Raynor's prediction had been spot-on.

Argentina had qualified for the finals and was one of the favorites, as they had won the South American Championship the year before. However, the Argentines had lost many of their best players to Italian football and were a much weakened team. One win and two losses, including a crushing loss to Czechoslovakia, resulted in them catching the first plane back home, where they were greeted with garbage and stones by disappointed fans.

Two of the remaining South American teams,

Paraguay and Mexico, also returned home after the first round of games, leaving Brazil as the sole representative from South America.

This was the only time all four British associations have been represented in the finals. Neither of the two more favored teams, England and Scotland, survived the opening round. England had sadly lost Duncan Edwards, Roger Byrne, and Tommy Taylor, three of its most influential players, in the Munich air crash only a few months earlier, but still fielded a team good enough to hold the mighty Brazilians to a goalless draw—surprisingly the first such scoreline in the history of the competition.

Northern Ireland enjoyed an excellent first round, never expecting to progress very far. They beat the Czechs 1–0, lost to Argentina, and drew with West Germany—although they had been just 10 minutes away from a famous victory.

In the play-offs for the group-qualifying games, Wales, a surprising but deserving qualifier, did well to overcome the Hungarians 2–1, while Northern Ireland beat Czechoslovakia by the same margin. However, hopes of having three British countries in the quarterfinals were dashed when England was beaten by the Soviet Union (which was competing for the first time) in a play-off, with the superb goalkeeping of Lev Yashin thwarting England's best efforts.

Wales gave what was probably their finest performance against Brazil. Their well-disciplined defense held the likes of Garrincha, Pele, and Didi until the 73d minute, when a goal by Pele, his first in the World Cup, sealed victory for the South Americans.

In the first semifinal, Sweden faced the champions, West Germany. Schafer gave the West Germans the lead midway through the first half, but with the crowd getting behind them, Sweden pressed forward and tied the game after 30 minutes. Angry scenes developed when the West German defender Juskowiak was sent off after nearly an hour. Sweden exploited their numerical advantage, and nine minutes from time Gren put the Swedes in front. Hamrin still had time to make it 3–1, and the crowd went wild with excitement.

In the other semifinal, favorite Brazil faced France, which had delighted the crowds with the outstanding goal-scoring achievements of Juste Fontaine, who finished as top scorer with a record 13 goals.

Brazil's supremacy was undisputed. They had arrived with a fresh, exciting team and new stars Garrincha, Vava, and Pele joined the great Santos and Didi. Vava joined the team for Brazil's second game with Garrincha (who had been born with a deformed leg), and Pele was selected for the third. But it was in the semifinal that Pele came into his own. On the way to a 5–2 victory he scored a hat trick in the space of just over 20 minutes—the last of which was a perfect volley from just outside the penalty area.

In the final, Brazil met the determined Swedes in front of a crowd of 50,000. George Raynor predicted that an early Swedish goal would throw Brazil into panic, but after Liedholm had indeed put the Swedes into a fourth-minute lead Raynor's predictive powers evaporated. Within six minutes, Vava equalized, and Brazil turned on the samba magic. Vava scored a second and then, 10 minutes into the second half, Pele controlled a difficult ball and flicked the ball over a defender's head before volleying it into the net. The Swedes went further behind before pulling a goal back, but it was only a matter of time before Zagalo (who was to manage Brazil in 1970) found the net again, to make the final score 5–2.

The World Cup was Brazil's at last. They became the only country to win the tournament outside their own continent and, as if to sum up the great spirit of the competition, they did a lap of honor around the stadium carrying the Swedish flag.

GROUP ONE

Northern Ireland	1	Czechoslovakia	0
West Germany	3	Argentina	1
Argentina	3	Northern Ireland	1
Czechoslovakia	2	West Germany	2
Northern Ireland	2	West Germany	2
Czechoslovakia	6	Argentina	1

FINAL TABLE

	Played	Won	Drawn	Lost	Goals For	Goals Against	Pts.
West Germany	3	1	2	0	7	5	4
Czechoslovakia	3	1	1	1	8	4	3
Northern Ireland	3	1	1	1	4	5	3
Argentina	3	1	0	2	5	10	2

Play-off: Northern Ireland   2   Czechoslovakia   1

GROUP TWO

Scotland	1	Yugoslavia	1
France	7	Paraguay	3
Paraguay	3	Scotland	2
Yugoslavia	3	France	2
France	2	Scotland	1
Paraguay	3	Yugoslavia	3

FINAL TABLE

	Played	Won	Drawn	Lost	Goals For	Goals Against	Pts.
France	3	2	0	11	1	7	4
Yugoslavia	3	1	2	0	7	6	4
Paraguay	3	1	1	1	9	12	3
Scotland	3	0	1	2	4	6	1

GROUP THREE

Sweden	3	Mexico	0
Hungary	1	Wales	1
Mexico	1	Wales	1
Sweden	2	Hungary	1
Sweden	0	Wales	0
Hungary	4	Mexico	0

FINAL TABLE

	Played	Won	Drawn	Lost	Goals For	Goals Against	Pts.
Sweden	3	2	1	0	5	1	5
Hungary	3	1	1	1	6	3	3
Wales	3	0	3	0	2	2	3
Mexico	3	0	1	2	1	8	1

Play-off: Wales 2 Hungary 1

GROUP FOUR

England	2	Soviet Union	2
Brazil	3	Austria	0
Soviet Union	2	Austria	0
Brazil	0	England	0
Austria	2	England	2
Brazil	2	Soviet Union	0

FINAL TABLE

	Played	Won	Drawn	Lost	Goals For	Goals Against	Pts.
Brazil	3	2	1	0	5	0	5
England	3	0	3	0	4	4	3
Soviet Union	3	1	1	1	4	4	3
Austria	3	0	1	2	2	7	1

Play-off: Soviet Union 1   England 0

QUARTERFINALS

France	4	Northern Ireland	0
West Germany	1	Yugoslavia	0
Sweden	2	Soviet Union	0
Brazil	1	Wales	0

SEMIFINALS

Sweden	3	West Germany	1
Brazil	5	France	2

THIRD-PLACE PLAY-OFF

France	6	West Germany	3

FINAL

| Brazil | 5 | Sweden | 2 |

Top goal-scorers: 13 Fontaine (France); 6 Pele (Brazil); 6 Rahn (West Germany); 5 McParland (Northern Ireland); 5 Vava (Brazil).

Fastest goal: 90 seconds, Vava (Brazil vs. France).

Most goals scored: 23 France.

Total goals scored: 126 (average 3.60 per game).

Total attendance: 868,000 (average 24,800 per game).

Final attendance: 49,737.

CHILE 1962

It was remarkable that Chile should successfully host the 1962 tournament, as earthquakes had devastated the country at the time when FIFA was considering the various candidates. But a desperate plea from Carlos Dittborn, the Chilean FA president, saying, "We must have the World Cup because we have nothing," seemed to do the trick, and the Chileans quickly started work on a magnificent new stadium in Santiago. Sadly, Dittborn died a month before the tournament he had done so much to organize. It was thanks to him that Chile proved to be such worthy hosts.

The format of the finals was similar to 1958, with four groups of four countries each playing one another and the top two progressing to the second round.

The winner in 1958 and now playing on South American soil, Brazil was inevitably the favorite. The team had changed very little in the four intervening years, but Pele's tournament was to be cut cruelly short through injury. Amarildo proved a marvelous replacement for the irreplaceable, but the finals belonged to his teammate Garrincha, whose dribbling skills, speed, and accuracy were a constant threat to every defense.

Brazil's strongest challenger was expected to be the Soviet Union, which opened their campaign with a 2–0 win over Yugoslavia in Group One. This was the first of several violent games in the tournament, but despite this both teams played some skillful football. The Russians were then involved in an extraordinary game against newcomer Colombia. Russia raced to a 3–0 lead after only 11 minutes, but the South Americans staged an exciting comeback to level the score at 4–4.

Qualification to the next round was ensured with a victory over Uruguay—no longer a dominant force in world soccer.

The hosts got off to a dreadful start in Group Two, losing a goal to Switzerland inside the opening 10 minutes of their first game. The crowd had to wait until just before halftime before they equalized, and Chile eventually won the game, 3–1. Chile's next match, against Italy, was probably one of the darkest chapters in the history of the World Cup. Dubbed the Battle of Santiago, it was reminiscent of the infamous Battle of Berne in 1954.

The root of the trouble was newspaper features written by Italian journalists criticizing the organization of the tournament and criticizing the squalor of Chile and Santiago in particular.

From the start, the Italian players were booed by the crowd and spat at and fouled by the Chilean players. After only eight minutes, Ferrini of Italy was sent off for retaliating after a bad tackle, but for 10 minutes Ferrini refused to leave the field. With both teams trading vicious fouls it was only a matter of time before the millions of viewers around the world witnessed more ugly scenes. After a bad tackle by the Italian Maschio on Sanchez, the Chilean responded by breaking the Italian's nose. Amazingly, neither one was sent off. The catalogue of disasters continued as Mario David became the second Italian to be given his marching orders. Even reduced to nine men, Italy held out until 15 minutes before time when, two late goals saw them effectively out of the finals.

Brazil and Czechoslovakia qualified comfortably from Group Three, although it was in their game that Pele sustained a muscle injury that ruled him out of the rest of the tournament. On a lighter note, the surprise result of the group found Mexico finally winning their first game in 14 World Cup matches.

Brazil's quarterfinal opponent was England, whose best performance thus far had been a 3–1 victory over Argentina. It was their misfortune to be drawn against the favorites with Garrincha, in devastating form, scoring twice in a 3–1 win.

Russia's progress was halted, surprisingly, by the hosts. Both goals in Chile's 2–1 victory were long-range shots and Lev Yashin, the Russian goalkeeper and one of the best in the world, if not of all time, would normally have saved both efforts comfortably. Not that this mattered to the jubilant Chileans, who had progressed farther than even they could possibly have hoped.

While Yashin was having a torrid time for the Soviet Union, Czechoslovakia's goalkeeper, Schroiff, was in brilliant form against the mighty Hungarians. After going a goal down early in the first half, the Hungarians threw everything at the Czech goal, inflicting serious damage to the woodwork. But the Czechs, the surprise team of the tournament, were well-organized and remained solid in defense.

The fourth quarterfinal, between Yugoslavia and West Germany, appeared to be heading inexorably toward extra time after an absorbing game when Radakovic, his head bandaged following a collision, scored from the edge of the penalty area with minutes left.

The most emotional of the semifinals involved the hosts and champions. Chile had surprised many people by reaching the semifinals but now they had to face Garrincha who took it upon himself to win the game. In the 9th minute he rifled in a fierce left-foot shot and added a second with a header. To their credit, Chile fought back and scored from a free kick, only for Vava to restore Brazil's two-goal advantage. Chilean hopes were again raised when Sanchez scored from the penalty spot, but Brazil was not to be denied their second successive final, and Vava once again headed in. The final few minutes deteriorated and Garrincha was sent off for retaliating and kicking Rojas. He faced suspension from the final.

In contrast, the semifinal game between Yugoslavia and Czechoslovakia attracted less than 6,000 people. The Czech goalkeeper, Schroiff, again made important saves, but the Czechs took their chances well, scoring three goals, conceding one.

After Chile won the third-place play-off, world attention turned to the final. Needless to say, Brazil was the hot favorite, but the Czechs were used to the underdog status by now. They were a fine athletic team, inspired by the all-around excellence of Masopust.

After his dismissal in the semifinal, Garrincha could count himself lucky that FIFA only issued a warning and that he was allowed to play in the final.

As in 1958, Brazil conceded the first goal, this time to the excellent Masopust, who calmly scored after receiving a long pass from Scherer. It took only two minutes for Brazil to level the score, with Amarildo beating the previously reliable Schroiff with a swerving shot from an acute angle. The Czechs were proving sturdy opposition for the favorites until the 68th minute, when Amarildo crossed the ball for Zito to score with a powerful header, and Schroiff's personal misery was compounded when he misjudged a high cross, lost control of the ball, and watched Vava tuck the ball into the net.

Brazil was a worthy winner.

GROUP ONE

Uruguay	2	Colombia	1
Soviet Union	2	Yugoslavia	0
Yugoslavia	3	Uruguay	1
Soviet Union	4	Colombia	4
Soviet Union	2	Uruguay	1
Yugoslavia	5	Colombia	0

FINAL TABLE

	Played	Won	Drawn	Lost	Goals For	Goals Against	Pts.
Soviet Union	3	2	1	0	8	5	5
Yugoslavia	3	2	0	1	8	3	4
Uruguay	3	1	0	2	4	6	2
Colombia	3	0	1	2	5	11	1

GROUP TWO

Chile	3	Switzerland	1
Italy	0	West Germany	0
Chile	2	Italy	0
West Germany	2	Switzerland	1
West Germany	2	Chile	0
Italy	3	Switzerland	0

FINAL TABLE

	Played	Won	Drawn	Lost	Goals For	Goals Against	Pts.
West Germany	3	2	1	0	4	1	5
Chile	3	2	0	1	5	3	4
Italy	3	1	1	1	3	2	3
Switzerland	3	0	0	3	2	8	0

GROUP THREE

Brazil	2	Mexico	0
Czechoslovakia	1	Spain	0
Brazil	0	Czechoslovakia	0
Spain	1	Mexico	0
Brazil	2	Spain	1
Mexico	3	Czechoslovakia	1

FINAL TABLE

	Played	Won	Drawn	Lost	Goals For	Goals Against	Pts.
Brazil	3	2	1	0	4	1	5
Czecho-slovakia	3	1	1	1	2	3	3
Mexico	3	1	0	2	3	4	2
Spain	3	1	0	2	2	3	2

GROUP FOUR

Argentina	1	Bulgaria	0
Hungary	2	England	1
England	3	Argentina	1
Hungary	6	Bulgaria	1
Argentina	0	Hungary	0
Bulgaria	0	England	0

FINAL TABLE

	Played	Won	Drawn	Lost	Goals For	Goals Against	Pts.
Hungary	3	2	1	0	8	2	5
England	3	1	1	1	4	3	3
Argentina	3	1	1	1	2	3	3
Bulgaria	3	0	1	2	1	7	1

QUARTERFINALS

Chile	2	Soviet Union	1
Yugoslavia	1	West Germany	0
Brazil	3	England	1
Czechoslovakia	1	Hungary ?	0

SEMIFINALS

Brazil	4	Chile	2
Czechoslovakia	3	Yugoslavia	1

THIRD-PLACE PLAY-OFF

Chile	1	Yugoslavia	0

FINAL

Brazil	3	Czechoslovakia	1

Top goal-scorers: 4 Albert (Hungary); 4 Garrincha (Brazil); 4 Ivanov (Soviet Union); 4 Jerkovic (Yugoslavia); 4 Sanchez (Chile); 4 Vava (Brazil).

Fastest goal: 1 minute, Albert (Hungary vs. Bulgaria); Masek (Czechoslovakia vs. Mexico).

Most goals scored: 14 Brazil.

Total goals scored: 89 (average 2.78 per game).

Total attendance: 776,000 (average 24,250 per game).

Final attendance: 68,679.

ENGLAND 1966

Despite meticulous organization by the English Football Association the 1966 tournament got off to a farcical start.

The first drama of the tournament started four months before a ball was kicked. The Jules Rimet Trophy was stolen on March 20 while on display at an exhibition at Westminster's Central Hall. Faced with the prospect of starting the tournament without a trophy, the FA called in Scotland Yard. But it was a black-and-white mongrel, Pickles, who sniffed out the cup in a South London garden one week later, saving the FA from further embarrassment.

In the early stages, the tournament was not distinguished by the overall quality of its football. In Group One, England, despite drawing a dull opening game against Uruguay, went on to beat Mexico and France to top their group without ever really showing what they were truly capable of. West Germany safely negotiated Group Two with the talented 20-year-old Franz Beckenbauer scoring two goals against Switzerland.

Group Three was by far the best of the World Cup sections with Brazil, Hungary, Portugal, and Bulgaria. Brazil had stayed faithful to its experienced players, including Pele who, at 25, was at the peak of his career.

Having beaten Bulgaria 2–0, Brazil faced Hungary, who had lost their opening game to the Portuguese. The teams served up a classic encounter, with the Hungarians displaying the sort of football that had made them such a powerful team in the 1950s. In fact the game went a long way from dispelling the ugly memories from the last time these teams had met in the so-called Battle of Berne 12 years before. Again the Hungarians came out on top, inflicting the first defeat in 13 World Cup games on the Brazilians.

Facing the prosect of not qualifying for the next stage, Brazil made nine changes for their match against Portugal, including the return of Pele, who was not fully fit from a knee injury sustained against Bulgaria in the opening match. However, the Portuguese were superior in most areas of the field and, once again, Pele was subjected to some harsh tackling that left him a hobbling spectator for much of the game. Afterward, Pele threatened never to play in another World Cup game and announced, "I don't want to finish my life as an invalid."

The team that captured the hearts of the crowd was undoubtedly the brave underdog North Korea. Hugely popular, the North Koreans caused a sensation by beating Italy and went on to qualify with the Soviet Union from Group Four. For Italy it was the ultimate humiliation. Twice winner of the trophy, the disgraced team was greeted on their return home with a bombardment of rotten vegetables from disappointed fans.

Having produced the shock of the tournament, the North Koreans seemed intent on making life hard for another of the tournament favorites, Portugal, in the quarterfinals. No one could have dreamt that after only 22 minutes the scoreline would read Portugal 0, North Korea 3, but it did. The North Koreans were waltzing around the Portuguese at will, but continued to play attacking football. This turned out to be their downfall, and eventually Eusebio took charge and almost single-handedly demolished the North Koreans, scoring two goals before halftime and another two before Augusto added a fifth to see Portugal into the semifinal—but not before they had had the fright of their lives.

England met Argentina in an eventful game. From the start Argentina delivered a number of nasty and deliberate fouls, and it was only a matter of time before the referee would send someone off. After a fierce tackle, the Argentinian captain Rattin was ordered off the field but refused to go. It was about 10 minutes before he finally left and the match could be restarted. England's Geoff Hurst scored the only goal in the second half of the ill-tempered match to book England's semifinal place, despite a poor display.

West Germany and the Soviet Union met in the first semifinal, and in a tough, physical match the otherwise excellent Soviet team lost their discipline. Chislenko was sent off, and his teammate Sabo spent most of the second half injured, as first Haller, then Beckenbauer scored before Porkujan pulled a goal back for the Russians.

By contrast, the other semifinal was full of attacking play, with two memorable goals from Bobby Charlton, the second of which was applauded even by some of the Portuguese players. Nobby Stiles shadowed Eusebio, preventing him from exerting the sort of deadly influence that had brought the Portuguese this far. Eusebio did manage to score from the penalty spot, but England survived an anxious final few minutes to win their first appearance in a World Cup final.

And what a final it was: one of the most televised, photographed, discussed matches in football history.

West Germany took the lead in the 12th minute when a poor clearance fell to Haller, who drove his shot past Gordon Banks. Geoff Hurst equalized with a header six minutes later, after which the game remained in deadlock. Franz Beckenbauer's influence was reduced, as he had specific orders to mark Bobby Charlton. This seemed decisive when England took the lead through Martin Peters. The whole of Wembley Stadium willed the referee to blow his whistle to end the game, but in a last-minute scramble from a West German free kick Weber stabbed the ball into the English net. The whole country was stunned.

The English manager, Alf Ramsey, inspired his team to greater efforts in extra time, which paid off when Alan Ball crossed the ball for Geoff Hurst to strike. The ball hit the underside of the crossbar, bounced straight down, and spun away from the goal. The English players appealed that it was a goal, while the Germans insisted that it had not crossed the line. The referee was not sure but after consulting his linesman he pointed to the center spot, and England was ahead 3–2. England's victory was sealed in the very last minute of the match, when Hurst broke free to become the only man to score a hat trick in a World Cup final.

WORLD CUP MEMORY

● ● ● ● ● ● ● ● ● ● ● ● ● ● ● ● ● ● ● ●

Roger Hunt, English striker:

"The natural instinct of a striker is to follow up a shot if there is the slightest doubt in his mind it isn't a goal. I was certain the ball had gone over the line; in fact I expected it to bounce up into the roof of the net. It was a shock when it came out again. Admittedly it would have ended all arguments if I had netted the ball, but to be honest, having watched it a thousand time on TV replays, I don't think I'd have got to it. The ball bounced off to the left and Weber, who was marking me, would have got there first."

When Germany equalized with only seconds to go Hunt's immediate thoughts were: "I was terribly dejected. Alf Ramsey came out onto the field and told us that we had won the World Cup once and that we could win it again. I remember Alan Ball placing the ball back on the center spot again. Seeing him so keen helped us all.

"Even so, it was a fantastic relief when Geoff Hurst got the fourth goal. There was no way the Germans could come back at us again."

● ●

GROUP ONE

England	0	Uruguay	0
France	1	Mexico	1
Uruguay	2	France	1
England	2	Mexico	0
Mexico	0	Uruguay	0
England	2	France	0

FINAL TABLE

	Played	Won	Drawn	Lost	Goals For	Goals Against	Pts.
England	3	2	1	0	4	0	5
Uruguay	3	1	2	0	2	1	4
Mexico	3	0	2	1	1	3	2
France	3	0	1	2	2	5	1

GROUP TWO

West Germany	5	Switzerland	0
Argentina	2	Spain	1
Spain	2	Switzerland	1
Argentina	0	West Germany	0
Argentina	2	Switzerland	0
West Germany	2	Spain	1

FINAL TABLE

	Played	Won	Drawn	Lost	Goals For	Goals Against	Pts.
West Germany	3	2	1	0	7	1	5
Argentina	3	2	1	0	4	1	5
Spain	3	1	0	2	4	5	2
Switzerland	3	0	0	3	1	9	0

GROUP THREE

Brazil	2	Bulgaria	0
Portugal	3	Hungary	1
Hungary	3	Brazil	1
Portugal	3	Bulgaria	0
Portugal	3	Brazil	1
Hungary	3	Bulgaria	1

FINAL TABLE

	Played	Won	Drawn	Lost	Goals For	Goals Against	Pts.
Portugal	3	3	0	0	9	2	6
Hungary	3	2	0	1	7	5	4
Brazil	3	1	0	2	4	6	2
Bulgaria	3	0	0	3	1	8	0

GROUP FOUR

Soviet Union	3	North Korea	0
Italy	2	Chile	0
Chile	1	North Korea	1
Soviet Union	1	Italy	0
North Korea	1	Italy	0
Soviet Union	2	Chile	1

FINAL TABLE

	Played	Won	Drawn	Lost	Goals For	Goals Against	Pts.
Soviet Union	3	3	0	0	6	1	6
North Korea	3	1	1	1	2	4	3
Italy	3	1	0	2	2	2	2
Chile	3	0	1	2	2	5	1

QUARTERFINALS

England	1	Argentina	0
West Germany	4	Uruguay	0
Portugal	5	North Korea	3
Soviet Union	2	Hungary	1

SEMIFINALS

West Germany	2	Soviet Union	1
England	2	Portugal	1

THIRD-PLACE PLAY-OFF

Portugal	2	Soviet Union	1

FINAL

England   4   West Germany 2
                                        (after extra time)

Top goal-scorers: 9 Eusebio (Portugal); 5 Haller (West Germany); 4 Beckenbauer (West Germany); 4 Bene (Hungary); 4 Hurst (England); 4 Porkujan (Soviet Union).

Fastest goal: 1 minute, Pak Seung-zin (North Korea vs. Portugal).

Most goals scored: 17 Portugal.

Total goals scored: 89 (average 2.78 per game).

Total attendance: 1,614,677 (average 50,458 per game).

Final attendance: 96,000.

MEXICO 1970

The decision to award the 1970 World Cup to Mexico was taken by FIFA at its Congress in Tokyo at the 1964 Olympic Games. However, many people were unhappy with the choice of venue because of the potential problems caused by Mexico's high altitude and heat. Watching Olympic athletes struggle in the 1968 Games in Mexico City did nothing to dispel these fears, and the decision to play some of the games at 12 noon, to fit in with peak viewing for European countries, only made matters worse.

As it turned out, the 1970 tournament was perhaps the best ever to be staged.

The competition was played in exactly the same format as in 1966, with four groups of four leading straight to the quarterfinals, but, for the first time, substitutions were introduced.

England set out for Mexico with a team capable of retaining the Cup they had won four years ago. The 4-3-3 system they had used in 1966 had become the more defensive 4-4-2; Banks was still in goal; the attack was augmented by Lee and Mullery, and Bobby Moore was at the peak of his career. Moore, unaffected by an attempt to frame him for the theft of a bracelet in Bogota, led England superbly, and a final against Brazil was widely predicted.

Brazil for its part was now managed by Zagalo, one of the stars of the 1958 and 1962 teams. Pele was now at his peak and with the exciting Tostao, Jairzinho, and Carlos Alberto, this was a team of great attacking flair.

Of the other qualifers, West Germany was eager to go one better than four years previously with the graceful

Beckenbauer and Overath in midfield and a new scoring sensation, Gerd Muller, in attack. Italy also possessed a striker of great goal-scoring talent named Luigi Riva. However, the Italian team was not considered strong enough to progress far, and Italian hopes were pinned on Riva having an exceptional tournament.

With Uruguay also qualifying for the finals, it was decided that should any of the three teams win the trophy for a third time, they should be allowed to retain it.

There was none of the violence that had undermined the game in the two previous tournaments. Not one player was even sent off, equaling the achievement of 1950.

The opening game of the tournament between Mexico and the Soviet Union ended goalless, like its 1966 counterpart. These two teams qualifed from Group One, but not until Mexico had benefited from a series of controversial refereeing decisions in their games against both El Salvador and Belgium. However, they were through to the knock-out phase, to the delight of the home support.

Group Two produced a couple of dull, dreary games. The Italians scored only one goal in three matches, beating Sweden 1–0 and drawing against Israel and Uruguay, who were lucky to qualify.

England opened their challenge against Romania, winning 1–0 thanks to a goal from the 1966 final hero, Geoff Hurst. Brazil faced Czechoslovakia with a talented lineup but, as has happened so frequently, it was their opponents that opened the scoring. This was perhaps what the Brazilians needed, and Rivelino equalized with a free kick that he bent around the defensive wall. Brazil eventually strolled to a 4–1 victory with two goals from Jairzinho and one from Pele, but it was a shot from Pele, on which he narrowly failed to score that is best remembered. He spotted Czech goalkeeper Viktor was well out of his goal, and from just inside his own half lofted a high ball over the goalkeeper's head that bounced inches wide of the goal.

The meeting between England and Brazil was eagerly anticipated and resulted in a classic game, played in intense heat that would have been a fitting finale to the tournament.

Brazil was without the influential Gerson, while England was missing Newton. For the English players there was the added disadvantage of suffering a disturbed night as a result of hundreds of Mexican fans singing and honking their horns outside their hotel.

Despite these problems and the debilitating effects of heat and altitude, England outplayed Brazil for long periods of the game. Bobby Moore was cool and creative in defense, and even Pele was kept quiet, although he had a fierce and well-directed header miraculously saved by England's goalkeeper, Gordon Banks—a save that is universally considered as the best seen.

Both teams had chances to win the game, but it was Tostao's splendid run and pass to Pele, who in turn laid the ball beautifully into the path of Jairzinho to score, that proved to be the match-winner. Despite England's 1–0 loss, this was reckoned to be just a prelude to the final.

In Group Four, Peru was coached by Didi, the Brazilian star of 1958 and 1962. However, their opening game against Bulgaria was shrouded in tragedy. A minute's silence was observed in memory of the thousands of people who had lost their lives in the Peruvian earthquake only two days before.

Against this background, it was perhaps understandable that Peru, one of the fancied outsiders, went two goals down. But they staged a remarkable comeback, and after two shrewd substitutions they hit back immediately with a goal from Gallardo. Five minutes later, Chumpitaz equalized from a free kick, and the impressive Cubillas completed the recovery with a brilliant solo effort.

The following day on the same ground, Morocco gave West Germany a fright. The North Africans fully deserved their lead after 21 minutes and it took the Germans until the 56th minute before they could equalize with intense pressure. A draw would have been a fair result, but 12 minutes from time, Gerd Muller, ever dangerous, scored his first World Cup goal.

Muller immediately added to his tally with a hat trick against Bulgaria and completed a second successive hat trick in the 3–1 defeat of Peru. However, both teams had already qualified.

The quarterfinals threw up a repeat of the 1966 final, pitching England against West Germany. Undoubtedly the most significant factor in the game happened the day before, when the utterly dependable Gordon Banks came down with an upset stomach. Peter Bonetti replaced him in the England goal but his performance would dog him for the rest of his career.

The match began well for England, with Mullery and Peters giving them a 2–0 lead after 50 minutes. Beckenbauer got a goal back for the Germans, a low shot that crept under Bonetti's body, but Alf Ramsey, the English manager, felt confident enough to substitute his most creative player, Bobby Charlton, to save him for the semifinals. It has always been seen as a crucial mistake. Meanwhile the West Germans also made a tactical substitution, bringing on Grabowski who, with his fresh legs, tormented Cooper in the English defense. Seeler equalized for West Germany, and Muller got the winner in extra time. Bonetti did not escape blame for either goal and never played for England again. It was also a sorry end for what was to be Bobby Charlton's last game for England.

After scoring only one goal in three matches, Italy quadrupled their tally against Mexico, with Riva getting two. However, it was not until the second-half substitution, which brought on the inspirational Rivera, that Italy gained the advantage for good.

Brazil also scored four in their dazzling victory over Peru. Gerson and Rivelino returned for Brazil, but it was Tostao who did the most damage, although errors by Felix, the Brazilian goalkeeper, gave Peru a brief glimmer of hope.

The semifinals pitted old foes Brazil and Uruguay, who had beaten the Soviet Union, and Italy against West Germany. Uruguay registered a complaint that Brazil was playing at Guadalajara once again and that the game should be moved. Their protest was to no avail.

Nonetheless, they took the lead—with Felix again responsible for not covering his angles properly in the Brazilian goal—and held it until late in the first half when Clodoaldo equalized. Brazil started the second half well, and Felix atoned for his previous mistake with a stunning save on Cubilla. With 14 minutes to go, Jairzinho waltzed past defenders, exchanged passes with Pele and Tostao, and drove the ball home. With seconds remaining, Rivelino crashed home a third from Pele's lovely pass, and Brazil was a finalist once again.

In Mexico City, a thrilling and fluctuating match took place between Italy and West Germany. This was by no means a classic encounter, but there were goals galore. Not that there was any hint of this as Italy grimly held on to their 7th-minute lead for the best part of the match, only for Schnellinger to grab an equalizer three minutes into injury time. Now came extra time and one of the most enduring World Cup images, that of Franz Beckenbauer playing on with his arm heavily strapped.

Muller—who else—scored inside five minutes of the start of extra time, but goals by Burgnich and Riva restored Italy's lead. With 10 minutes to go, Muller tied the match with his 10th goal of the competition, but Rivera scored virtually from the restart, and not even the resilient West Germans could come back again. They had played two tiring games, both of which had gone into extra time.

So it was Brazil versus Italy in the final, and whoever won would be the permanent holder of the Jules Rimet Trophy. Pele opened the scoring with a spectacular jump and header from a cross by Rivelino. Eight minutes before the interval, Boninsega pounced on a defensive lapse and equalized. If Italy could have pressed home their psychological advantage at this point then the game might have taken a different course. But Brazil regained control, and Gerson pivoted to hit a fierce, low drive past Albertosi in the Italian goal. From this point, Brazil turned on a magical display. Gerson's cross was headed down by Pele for Jairzinho to create World Cup history by scoring in every round.

The fourth goal was also one to savor. Jairzinho found Pele, who laid the ball immaculately to his right for Carlos Alberto to drive the ball imperiously into the goal.

The celebrations were spectacular, with fans parading with their victorious players. Brazil had made the game look enjoyable to play and won the World Cup in glorious style.

WORLD CUP MEMORY

● ●

Rivelino, Brazilian striker:

"We never though we would get past the first round—having England in our group was a real damper on our spirits. But our trainer, Zagalo, showed us exactly what our movements should be and prepared us so well physically that we hardly felt any tiredness at all. The first game is always the most important, and our 4–1 victory over Czechoslovakia gave us the confidence to beat England 1–0, after which we knew we would win the tournament. During the final against Italy, I put the ball across for Pele for his first goal, and I also set up the goal Jairzinho scored, the third one. It was magic."

● ●

GROUP ONE

Mexico	0	Soviet Union	0
Belgium	3	El Salvador	0
Soviet Union	4	Belgium	1
Mexico	4	El Salvador	0
Soviet Union	2	El Salvador	0
Mexico	1	Belgium	0

FINAL TABLE

	Played	Won	Drawn	Lost	Goals For	Goals Against	Pts.
Soviet Union	3	2	1	0	6	1	5
Mexico	3	2	1	0	5	0	5
Belgium	3	1	0	2	4	5	2
El Salvador	3	0	0	3	0	9	0

GROUP TWO

Uruguay	2	Israel	0
Italy	1	Sweden	0
Uruguay	0	Italy	0
Israel	1	Sweden	1
Sweden	1	Uruguay	0
Israel	0	Italy	0

FINAL TABLE

	Played	Won	Drawn	Lost	Goals For	Goals Against	Pts.
Italy	3	1	2	0	1	0	4
Uruguay	3	1	1	1	2	1	3
Sweden	3	1	1	1	2	2	3
Israel	3	0	2	1	1	3	2

GROUP THREE

England	1	Romania	0
Brazil	4	Czechoslovakia	1
Romania	2	Czechoslovakia	1
Brazil	1	England	0
Brazil	3	Romania	2
England	1	Czechoslovakia	0

FINAL TABLE

	Played	Won	Drawn	Lost	Goals For	Goals Against	Pts.
Brazil	3	3	0	0	8	3	6
England	3	2	0	1	2	1	4
Romania	3	1	0	2	4	5	2
Czecho-slovakia	3	0	0	3	2	7	0

GROUP FOUR

Peru	3	Bulgaria	2
West Germany	2	Morocco	1
Peru	3	Morocco	0
West Germany	5	Bulgaria	2
West Germany	3	Peru	1
Bulgaria	1	Morocco	1

FINAL TABLE

	Played	Won	Drawn	Lost	Goals For	Goals Against	Pts.
West Germany	3	3	0	0	10	4	6
Peru	3	2	0	1	7	5	4
Bulgaria	3	0	1	2	5	9	1
Morocco	3	0	1	2	2	6	1

QUARTERFINALS

West Germany	3	England	2 (after extra time)
Italy	4	Mexico	1
Brazil	4	Peru	2
Uruguay	1	Soviet Union	0

SEMIFINALS

Italy	4	West Germany	3 (after extra time)
Brazil	3	Uruguay	1

THIRD-PLACE PLAY-OFF

West Germany	1	Uruguay	0

FINAL

Brazil	4	Italy	1

Top goal-scorers: 10 Muller (West Germany); 7 Jairzinho (Brazil); 5 Cubillas (Peru); 4 Bishovets (Soviet Union); 4 Pele (Brazil).

Fastest goal: 3 minutes, Petras (Czechoslovakia vs. Romania).

Most goals scored: 19 Brazil.

Total goals scored: 95 (average 2.97 per game).

Total attendance: 1,673,975 (average 52,312 per game).

Final attendance: 107,000.

WEST GERMANY 1974

West Germany was awarded the 10th World Cup tournament at FIFA's 1968 Congress so, like Mexico, West Germany had the honor of staging the Olympic Games and then the World Cup within two years of each other.

A few days before the opening ceremony, Joao Havelange succeeded Stanley Rous as president of FIFA. The tournament also had a new trophy, called simply the FIFA World Cup, to replace the original, which had been won outright by Brazil in 1970.

Many famous names were absent from the finals. England, Hungary, Czechoslovakia, and France—teams with a proud football heritage—all failed to qualify, but the most controversial absentee was the Soviet Union. Forced to play off against Chile, they tied the first leg in Moscow 0–0. They refused to play the return leg, to be staged in the National Stadium of Santiago, on the grounds that the stadium had been the scene of the murder of political prisoners, many of them communists, during the coup. After protracted meetings, FIFA ruled that the match should go ahead. Chile took to the field without the Russians, scored a goal, and qualified for the finals.

For the first time since 1950, the system of groups was extended beyond the first-round games. As before, 16 nations competed, divided into four groups of four, but instead of a second-round knock-out tournament, the top two teams went into further groups, with the winners becoming the finalists and the runners-up meeting in the third-place match.

West Germany, the European champion and host, was the obvious favorite and was drawn in Group One with Chile and newcomers East Germany and Australia. After two unconvincing victories by the host there was inevitable tension for the first-ever meeting between the two Germanies, and security was tight. The first half failed to produce a goal, although both sides came close. Though West Germany dominated the second half it was East Germany that scored with an opportunistic goal 10 minutes from time. The historic result meant that both teams qualifed, but by finishing second, West Germany avoided Holland in the second phase. Even so, the West Germans came under strong criticism for their lack-luster performances.

Brazil was no longer the same exciting team that had enthralled everyone four years before. There was no Pele, Tostao, or Gerson, and Brazil's new defensive style was much lamented. However, they qualified with Yugoslavia for the second round at the expense of Scotland and Zaire. Scotland, despite remaining unbeaten, went out on goal difference and only one goal at that. They had only scored two to Brazil's three against Zaire—neither of which approached the nine goals Yugoslavia put past the African team.

This tournament was the World Cup of "total foot-ball," the theory of which was that any player could do anything: attackers become defenders, defenders become attackers. It was not a form of tactics, but a style where players would not be limited to certain positions on the field. The team would be composed of highly skillful and versatile players, and the teams that were to demonstrate this to the best effect were West Germany and particu-larly Holland, who qualified for the second phase with Sweden.

In the final group, Italy made hard work of beating

Haiti. They went a goal down early in the second half, but goals from the experienced Rivera, Benetti, and Anastasi dispelled thoughts of a repeat of the nightmare of North Korea's win in 1966. On the same day, Argentina, which had been awarded the 1978 finals, faced Poland, one of the best teams in the tournament. In a good, open match, Poland scored two early goals, but had the young Mario Kempes scored in the opening minutes things might have been different. Kempes's day was to come four years later, but for now his team qualified with Poland.

The two second-phase groups were composed of Holland, Brazil, Argentina, and East Germany; and West Germany, Poland, Yugoslavia, and Sweden.

Brazil beat the East Germans, thanks to one of Rivelino's free-kick specials—his teammate Jairzinho stood in the East German defensive wall and ducked out of the way of Rivelino's fiercely struck shot.

Holland was getting better and better as the tournament progressed. Argentina was the next team that was powerless to stop Holland's irresistible attacking football as Cruyff scored two of the four goals in a virtuoso performance. But the Dutch were more than a one-man team, as they proved against East Germany. With Cruyff being closely marked by Weise, the Dutch still had enough firepower to score two goals to set up a decisive match against Brazil.

In a physical match, Brazil resorted to some dangerous tackles, with Holland often returning the treatment with interest. However, the game was saved by two brilliant strikes by Neeskens and Cruyff to send Holland into their first final.

The other second-round group saw a similar "decider" situation develop. Both Poland and West Germany won their first two matches, although the Germans knew they could rely on a draw in their final game.

West Germany was now looking like a potential champion. Against Yugoslavia they dominated much of the match, with Breitner scoring with a tremendous drive and Muller also getting on the score sheet. Just as importantly, Beckenbauer was back to his most majestic form. Improvement continued against Sweden in an entertaining game, as Muller played a leading role without actually scoring in the 4–2 win.

Poland had been less impressive and was considered fortunate to beat Yugoslavia and Sweden. The decisive match of the group was played on a rain-soaked field, but despite the atrocious conditions the game was an entertaining affair. Sepp Maier, the German goalkeeper, brought off an excellent save on Lato in the first half to keep the Germans in the game. Muller had been kept very quiet all game, but, with only 12 minutes to go, he snatched on to a half-chance to score the goal that saw the host team through to the final.

Holland kicked off in the final, and before a West German player had even touched the ball the Dutch were a goal up. A superb run by Cruyff ended up with him being fouled inside the penalty area by Hoeness. Neeskens scored from the penalty spot with barely a minute gone. For nearly half an hour, the Dutch played with the arrogance of a team that assumed they had won, and one can only assume that if they had pressed home their advantage they would have won.

After 25 minutes, however, Jack Taylor, the English referee, awarded the West Germans a more controversial penalty. Breitner brought the scores level and, after Rep had missed a simple chance to restore Holland's lead, Muller won the World Cup with a well-taken goal just before halftime. Cruyff was cautioned for arguing, but the Dutch only had themselves to blame for underestimating the opposition's powers of recovery.

Try as they might in the second half, the Dutch could not score, and for the second time the World Cup went to West Germany.

WORLD CUP MEMORY

● ●

Paul Breitner, West German defender:

"Going into the final we were confident we would win the World Cup because neither West Germany nor Holland was the best team in the tournament. The best team was Poland, whom we had beaten in the second round of matches.

"Probably the best thing to happen was that Holland scored in the first minute. A German player hadn't touched the ball and we were down 1-0. After the goal, the Dutch relaxed and played as if they thought they would win easily—we became stronger and stronger.When we were awarded the penalty, I knew straight away that I should be the player to take it. Muller, Beckenbauer, or Overath would normally have taken it but they all appeared unsure, so I grabbed the ball and took the responsibility. The goalkeeper moved to the left, so I placed it to the right."

● ●

GROUP ONE

West Germany	1	Chile	0
East Germany	2	Australia	0
West Germany	3	Australia	0
Chile	1	East Germany	1
East Germany	1	West Germany	0
Australia	0	Chile	0

FINAL TABLE

	Played	Won	Drawn	Lost	Goals For	Goals Against	Pts.
East Germany	3	2	1	0	4	1	5
West Germany	3	2	0	1	4	1	4
Chile	3	0	2	1	1	2	2
Australia	3	0	1	2	0	5	1

GROUP TWO

Brazil	0	Yugoslavia	0
Scotland	2	Zaire	0
Brazil	0	Scotland	0
Yugoslavia	9	Zaire	0
Scotland	1	Yugoslavia	1
Brazil	3	Zaire	0

FINAL TABLE

	Played	Won	Drawn	Lost	Goals For	Goals Against	Pts.
Yugoslavia	3	1	2	0	1	0	4
Brazil	3	1	2	0	3	0	4
Scotland	3	1	2	0	3	1	4
Zaire	3	0	0	3	0	14	0

GROUP THREE

Holland	2	Uruguay	0
Bulgaria	0	Sweden	0
Holland	0	Sweden	0
Bulgaria	1	Uruguay	1
Holland	4	Bulgaria	1
Sweden	3	Uruguay	0

FINAL TABLE

	Played	Won	Drawn	Lost	Goals For	Goals Against	Pts.
Holland	3	2	1	0	6	1	5
Sweden	3	1	2	0	3	0	4
Bulgaria	3	0	2	1	2	5	2
Uruguay	3	0	1	2	1	6	1

GROUP FOUR

Italy	3	Haiti	1
Poland	3	Argentina	2
Argentina	1	Italy	1
Poland	7	Haiti	0
Argentina	4	Haiti	1
Poland	2	Italy	1

FINAL TABLE

	Played	Won	Drawn	Lost	Goals For	Goals Against	Pts.
Poland	3	3	0	0	12	3	6
Argentina	3	1	1	1	7	5	3
Italy	3	1	1	1	5	4	3
Haiti	3	0	0	3	2	14	0

GROUP A

Brazil	1	East Germany	0
Holland	4	Argentina	0
Holland	2	East Germany	0
Brazil	2	Argentina	1
Holland	2	Brazil	0
Argentina	1	East Germany	1

FINAL TABLE

	Played	Won	Drawn	Lost	Goals For	Goals Against	Pts.
Holland	3	3	0	0	8	0	6
Brazil	3	2	0	1	3	3	4
East Germany	3	0	1	2	1	4	1
Argentina	3	0	1	2	2	7	1

GROUP B

Poland	1	Sweden	0
West Germany	2	Yugoslavia	0
Poland	2	Yugoslavia	1
West Germany	4	Sweden	2
Sweden	2	Yugoslavia	1
West Germany	1	Poland	0

FINAL TABLE

	Played	Won	Drawn	Lost	Goals For	Goals Against	Pts.
West Germany	3	3	0	0	7	2	6
Poland	3	2	0	1	3	2	4
Sweden	3	1	0	2	4	6	2
Yugoslavia	3	0	0	3	2	6	0

THIRD-PLACE PLAY-OFF

Poland	1	Brazil	0

FINAL

West Germany	2	Holland	1

Top goal-scorers: 7 Lato (Poland); 5 Neeskens (Holland);
   5 Szarmach (Poland); 4 Edstrom (Sweden);
   4 Muller (West Germany); 4 Rep (Holland).
Fastest goal: 80 seconds, Neeskens (Holland vs. West Germany).
Most goals scored: 16 Poland.
Total goals scored: 97 (average 2.55 per game).
Total attendance: 1,774,022 (average 46,685 per game).
Final attendance: 77,833.

ARGENTINA 1978

There were grave doubts about whether the 1978 World
Cup should go ahead in Argentina, a country ruled by a
military junta headed by General Videla, who had ousted
Isabel Perón in 1976. After the coup, fears increased
when thousands of people were tortured or simply went
missing. The junta set up a body, the *Ente Autarquico
Mundial,* to ensure that all the preparations for the tournament were completed in time, but this looked unlikely
when its chief, General Actis, was assassinated. Yet
despite a background of terrorism and an unstable economy the tournament actually passed without a major
incident.

The chain-smoking Argentinian manager, Cesar
Menotti, having seen many of his country's best players
move to Europe, decided that the bulk of his team would
be home-based. But he did recall Mario Kempes from
Valencia in Spain—a decision that was ultimately to win
the World Cup.

Argentina made a winning if not sensational start to
its campaign with a 2–1 win over Hungary in what was a
tough qualifying group. They beat France, 2–1, in their
next game, but this was largely due to two outrageous
decisions by the referee. The first came from an incident
when the French defender Tresor tackled Kempes and
fell on the ball. The referee gave a penalty to Argentina,
but the reason was unclear. Surely it was not a deliberate
foul, and if Tresor had handled the ball, it was acciden-
tal. Passarella converted the penalty, and France did well
to fight back and equalize through Michel Platini. Luque
put Argentina back in front with a tremendous long-
range shot, but the French pushed forward and should

have been awarded a penalty themselves when Didier Six was brought down, but for this clear infringement the referee gave nothing.

Italy and Argentina were assured of qualification, but their game was important, as the winner of the group would stay in Buenos Aires. Argentina had their chances, but Italy's tight marking and solid defense gave Kempes few opportunities. Rossi instigated the winning goal, playing a smart one-two with Bettega, who scored.

The Group Two game between Poland and West Germany was the opening match of the tournament, and for the fourth successive time failed to provide any goals. With Lato, Deyna, and Boniek, Poland had an excellent team, whereas the West Germans desperately missed the likes of Muller and Beckenbauer. Both teams qualified as expected but were given a surprisingly tough time by Tunisia, who beat Mexico, lost narrowly to Poland, and held the West Germans to a goalless draw. Of the two teams, Tunisia created the better chances.

Brazil blundered their way through Group Three, enlivened by an extraordinary decision by referee Clive Thomas in their game against Sweden. With the score at 1–1, Zico headed home a corner to win the match, but as the ball was sailing into the net, Thomas blew his whistle for full time. The Brazilians were outraged, but Thomas stood by his decision. In the end Brazil qualified with Austria.

In Group Four, Peru shattered the illusions of Scotland by beating them 3–1 with Cubillas, a rising star in 1970, scoring two. The overconfident Scots were guilty of treating Peru too lightly, but after a miserable 1–1 draw with Iran they very nearly put out Holland. Scotland needed to win by three goals, and after Archie Gemmill had jinked his way through the Dutch defense to make it

3–1, they were within sight of that margin. Their hopes were short-lived, as Johnny Rep scored from 25 yards and Scotland went out for a second successive time on goal difference. One Scot, Willie Johnston, arrived home earlier than his teammates, having failed a dope test after the Peru game.

Group A in the second round consisted of Italy, West Germany, Holland, and Austria; Group B was made up of Argentina, Peru, Brazil, and Poland.

The opening game of Group A pitted Italy, winner of all their games, against West Germany. Italy had their chances, but the game finished goalless. On the same day, Holland tore into the Austrian defense, with Rep scoring twice and Brandts, Rensenbrink, and Willy van der Kerkhof completing an impressive 5–1 win. Goal difference would be used to determine the group winners in case of a tie, which rendered this score of huge importance.

As a result, West Germany had to forsake their defensive system against Holland, and although they went up on an early goal, Haan demonstrated his formidable shooting power from 30 yards to make the score even. Even the experienced Sepp Maier in the German goal could do nothing to stop the thunderbolt. West Germany reestablished their lead, but Rene van der Kerkhof (Willy's twin) threaded his way through the German defense to tie the game.

After Italy beat Austria, they knew they had to beat the Dutch to have a chance of reaching the final. Italy committed themselves to attack and took a first-half lead when Brandts put through his own goal while trying to clear the ball from danger. As well as giving away a goal, he caught the right knee of his goalkeeper, Jongbloed, who had to be substituted. The match was ill-tempered, but the best football was played by the Dutch, for whom Brandts atoned for his previous error by scoring from 20 yards. This paved the way for Haan to score another thunderous long-range effort from over 30 yards, and Holland was through to their second successive final.

In Group B, Brazil started to play the sort of football the fans expected in beating Peru. That evening, Mario Kempes scored twice against Poland as Argentina was spurred on by a fanatical crowd. This set up the crucial game between the South American favorites, and emotions were certainly running high as both teams were desperate to remain unbeaten. The game remained goalless, but four players were booked and four went off injured where no prisoners were taken.

The goalless scoreline left the group wide open, and Brazil was rightly furious that their game against Poland was to be played before Argentina's final game. With the group likely to be decided on goal difference, the hosts would know exactly how many goals they needed to win by.

Brazil put up their best performance to beat Poland 3–1, leaving Argentina needing to win by at least four goals. Grave doubts persisted about the validity of their 6–0 rout of Peru, doubts that they overran the opposition rather too easily, even though Peru hit a post early on. Luque scored two as did Kempes, taking his tally to four.

The crowds greeted Argentina for the final at the River Plata stadium with the now customary ticker-tape reception. However, the game was delayed by Argentine complaints about the strapping worn by Rene van der Kerkhof on an injured forearm. The Dutch, angered by what they saw as blatant gamesmanship, began over-physically, and it took the skill of Ardiles and the finishing power of Kempes to bring the match distinction. Kempes opened the scoring in the 38th minute, a lead they held until Nanninga headed the equalizer with less than 10 minutes to go. The Dutch pushed forward with renewed vigor, and Rensenbrink hit a post in the last minute. A shade the other way and the Dutch would have been champions. By such close margins are games decided. But it was not to be. Kempes scored his sixth goal of the tournament in the first period of extra time, forcing his way past three defenders, to make the score 2–1. And with five minutes left, and Holland committed to attack, Kempes played a neat one-two with Bertoni, who scored an easy third goal.

The stadium erupted in celebration and the streets of Buenos Aires were packed with ecstatic crowds. Holland had again lost to the host nation, but had contributed some exciting football in what had turned out to be a successful tournament.

GROUP ONE

Italy	2	France	1
Argentina	2	Hungary	1
Italy	3	Hungary	1
Argentina	2	France	1
Italy	1	Argentina	0
France	3	Hungary	1

FINAL TABLE

	Played	Won	Drawn	Lost	Goals For	Goals Against	Pts.
Italy	3	3	0	0	6	2	6
Argentina	3	2	0	1	4	3	4
France	3	1	0	2	5	5	2
Hungary	3	0	0	3	3	8	0

GROUP TWO

Poland	0	West Germany	0
Tunisia	3	Mexico	1
Poland	1	Tunisia	0
West Germany	6	Mexico	0
Tunisia	0	West Germany	0
Poland	3	Mexico	1

FINAL TABLE

	Played	Won	Drawn	Lost	Goals For	Goals Against	Pts.
Poland	3	2	1	0	4	1	5
West Germany	3	1	2	0	6	0	4
Tunisia	3	1	1	1	3	2	3
Mexico	3	0	0	3	2	12	0

GROUP THREE

Brazil	1	Sweden	1
Austria	2	Spain	1
Austria	1	Sweden	0
Brazil	0	Spain	0
Brazil	1	Austria	0
Spain	1	Sweden	0

FINAL TABLE

	Played	Won	Drawn	Lost	Goals For	Goals Against	Pts.
Austria	3	2	0	1	3	2	4
Brazil	3	1	2	0	2	1	4
Spain	3	1	1	1	2	2	3
Sweden	3	0	1	2	1	3	1

GROUP FOUR

Holland	3	Iran	0
Peru	3	Scotland	1
Holland	0	Peru	0
Iran	1	Scotland	1
Scotland	3	Holland	2
Peru	4	Iran	1

FINAL TABLE

	Played	Won	Drawn	Lost	Goals For	Goals Against	Pts.
Peru	3	2	1	0	7	2	5
Holland	3	1	1	1	5	3	3
Scotland	3	1	1	1	5	6	3
Iran	3	0	1	2	2	8	1

GROUP A

Italy	0	West Germany	0
Holland	5	Austria	1
Holland	2	West Germany	2
Italy	1	Austria	0
Holland	2	Italy	1
Austria	3	West Germany	2

FINAL TABLE

	Played	Won	Drawn	Lost	Goals For	Goals Against	Pts.
Holland	3	2	1	0	9	4	5
Italy	3	1	1	1	2	2	3
West Germany	3	0	2	1	4	5	2
Austria	3	1	0	2	4	8	2

GROUP B

Brazil	3	Peru	0
Argentina	2	Poland	0
Poland	1	Peru	0
Argentina	0	Brazil	0
Brazil	3	Poland	1
Argentina	6	Peru	0

FINAL TABLE

	Played	Won	Drawn	Lost	Goals For	Goals Against	Pts.
Argentina	3	2	1	0	8	0	5
Brazil	3	2	1	0	6	1	5
Poland	3	1	0	2	2	5	2
Peru	3	0	0	3	0	10	0

THIRD-PLACE PLAY-OFF

Brazil	2	Italy	1

FINAL

Argentina	3	Holland	1 (after extra time)

Top goal-scorers: 6 Kempes (Argentina); 5 Cubillas (Peru); 5 Rensenbrink (Holland); 4 Krankl (Austria); 4 Luque (Argentina).

Fastest goal: 31 seconds, Lacombe (France vs. Italy).

Most goals scored: 15 Argentina, Holland.

Total goals scored: 102 (average 2.68).

Total attendance: 1,610,215 (average 42,374 per game).

Final attendance: 77,260.

SPAIN 1982

The sweltering Spanish summer of 1982 saw the arrival of a young Argentine star, Diego Maradona. But his turn was to come; this tournament belonged to Paolo Rossi.

For the first time the number of finalists was enlarged from 16 to 24 to provide a more universal representation of nations. Because of the increased number of entrants another format was devised, with the 24 teams divided into six groups of four. The top two teams then went into four further groups of three, with the group winners progressing to a semifinal knock-out stage. This meant, in effect, that the teams had to qualify all over again, and there were concerns that this format might produce defensive, turgid games.

However, the tournament kicked off with a spectacular ceremony, and for the first time in 20 years the opening game, between Argentina and Belgium, produced a goal. The South Americans were showcasing a new superstar of world soccer, Diego Maradona, but he was brought down to earth by Belgium's uncompromising tactics. Despite frequently having all 11 men in defense, it was Belgium that scored with a rapid counterattack.

These two teams eventually qualified at the expense of Hungary and El Salvador. In their encounter, Hungary had beaten El Salvador 10–1, a score that fueled the argument of critics who were opposed to expanding the number of finalists. However, El Salvador tightened up their act against Belgium and were in fairness the only so-called 'weaker' football nation not to do themselves justice.

Africa was now represented by two teams—Cameroon and Algeria. Cameroon was drawn with Italy, Poland,

and Peru in Group One but was by no means overawed by its illustrious opponents. In a group that saw five tied games and only one win—Poland beating Peru—Cameroon was unfortunate not to qualify, only losing out by virtue of Italy having been involved in two 1–1 draws as opposed to Cameroon's one. But they left having played with disciplined flair, and had been one of the most charismatic teams in the tournament.

Algeria gave further proof that the emerging teams were not to be underestimated with perhaps the biggest upset in World Cup history. In their opening game in Gijon, they beat the mighty West Germany 2–1. In their second game the Algerians again took the initiative from the start but lost 2–0 to Austria, which had effectively qualified, having already beat Chile. West Germany's victory over Chile gave them the same point total as Algeria, so it all came down to the final matches. The lessons of the previous tournament had evidently not been learned, as Algeria's game against Chile was played a day before West Germany was due to meet Austria.

The Algerians once again gave a scintillating display and raced into an early 3–0 lead, but they tired as the match progressed and conceded two second-half goals. The next day witnessed one of the most disgraceful matches ever seen. A 1–0 win by West Germany would see them and Austria through, and after the Germans had scored, the game lost any meaning. The Algerians' appeal to FIFA was rejected.

In Group Four, England got off to a remarkable start against France when Bryan Robson scored after only 27 seconds to record the fastest-ever World Cup goal. Both teams qualified, England with a perfect record.

With the host nation having won the past two tournaments, Spain was considered one of the likely favorites.

Although their World Cup record was not particularly good, Spain boasted one of the best leagues in the world and a team of highly talented individuals. Sadly, only a dubious penalty saved them from defeat at the hands of Honduras, and they struggled to beat Yugoslavia with the help of another penalty. In their final group game, Spain faced the Irish, who needed a win to qualify. Spain could afford a defeat, but by no more than one goal, and once Armstrong had scored early in the second half, there was every chance that the hosts would face an early exit. They survived, but went into a tough group with West Germany and England.

Group Six was the best of the first round. Brazil was back to its exhilarating style of old, with fluent, attacking football and great individual skill. They fell a goal behind to the Soviet Union but never appeared to be troubled as first Socrates, then Eder scored tremendous goals. Scotland also took the lead against the South Americans, Narey scoring a goal any one of his opponents would have been delighted with. But Zico, Oscar, Eder, and Falcao restored order and put the game beyond Scotland's reach.

The four groups for the second round contained some interesting draws. Group C was particularly strong, with Brazil, Argentina, and Italy competing for a semifinal place. Italy gave their experienced defender Gentile the job of marking Maradona, who suffered from some rough tackles. However, after containing Argentina in the first half, Italy attacked in the second and scored twice before Passarella pulled one back for Argentina.

Worse was to come for the defending champions when they faced Brazil. This was truly a wonderful Brazilian team, and they totally outplayed Argentina, taking a 3–0 lead. Near the end, Maradona's frustration finally got the better of him and he kicked out at Batista. The referee had no hesitation in sending him off.

It was not to be Maradona's year, but the star of the tournament was about to make his mark. The decider between Brazil and Italy was a classic. It was a game Italy needed to win, and within 5 minutes Paolo Rossi had put them ahead. But Brazil was not worried, and in the 12th minute Socrates duly equalized with a brilliant solo goal. Rossi restored Italy's lead after 25 minutes following a defensive blunder, but Falcao pulled the scores level with 22 minutes remaining, and Brazil appeared set for the semifinals. Had they played more defensively, Brazil would surely have done so, but they continued to push forward, and 15 minutes from time Rossi completed a memorable hat trick and ensured Italy's victory.

Brazil was out, but they had been the most outstanding team of the tournament.

Group B was also very tight. After a drab, goalless draw against West Germany, England needed to beat Spain by two goals to win the group. But this was to be a night of near-misses and stout defending by the Spanish, and even the introduction of Kevin Keegan could not bring the vital goals England so desperately needed. So having conceded only one goal and having remained unbeaten throughout, England made a sad exit.

France had displayed some indifferent form at the beginning of the tournament, but they now began to play to the best of their ability. With Platini, Giresse, and Tigani in midfield they outplayed Austria and Northern Ireland to set up a semifinal against West Germany.

The first semifinal saw Italy meet Poland, which had qualified by virtue of scoring more goals against Belgium than the Soviet Union had managed. Italy was without

Gentile, but Poland was also without Boniek and it showed. Once again, Paolo Rossi was the inspiration, scoring both goals.

The game between France and West Germany was one of the all-time greats. Littbarski scored for the West Germans in the 18th minute, but nine minutes later France equalized from the penalty spot after Rocheteau had been brought down in the area. The score did not change for the remainder of normal time, although both teams had their chances, but a crucial incident took place that was ultimately to turn the game. Eight minutes after coming on as a substitute, Battiston, a French defender, was brought crashing to the ground by Schumacher, the West German goalkeeper. The Frenchman was carried off unconscious and Schumacher, remarkably, remained on the field.

Only two minutes into extra time, Tresor gave France the lead, and when Giresse made it 3–1 they were seemingly on their way to their first final. Had Battiston still been on the field he might have strengthened a weakening defense, but the West Germans took a gamble and brought on Karl-Heinz Rummenigge, who instigated West Germany's revival. For the first time in the World Cup penalties were used to decide a game, and with the score at 4–4, Schumacher saved from Bossis and Hrubesch put West Germany into the final.

Before the final, France and Poland were involved in one of those World Cup rarities—an entertaining third-place play-off, with Poland defeating a much-changed French team, 3–2.

Italy was a much-improved team from the one that had started the tournament with three draws. They were without Antognoni and after eight minutes were also minus Graziani, who damaged his shoulder. The first half was dominated by fouls, and Italian Antonio Cabrini wrote his name in the record books by becoming the first man to miss a penalty shot in a World Cup final.

It was bound to be Rossi who broke the deadlock. Twelve minutes into the second half, he rose to meet a cross from Gentile, and Italy was one up. After 68 minutes, Tardelli made it two with a scorching shot, and Altobelli made sure of victory nine minutes from time.

Breitner scored a consolation goal, but this was one occasion where the West Germans' famed resolve deserted them.

GROUP ONE

Italy	0	Poland	0
Cameroon	0	Peru	0
Italy	1	Peru	1
Cameroon	0	Poland	0
Poland	5	Peru	1
Cameroon	1	Italy	1

FINAL TABLE

	Played	Won	Drawn	Lost	Goals For	Goals Against	Pts.
Poland	3	1	2	0	5	1	4
Italy	3	0	3	0	2	2	3
Cameroon	3	0	3	0	1	1	3
Peru	3	0	2	1	2	6	2

GROUP TWO

Algeria	2	West Germany	1
Austria	1	Chile	0
West Germany	4	Chile	1
Austria	2	Algeria	0
Algeria	3	Chile	2
West Germany	1	Austria	0

FINAL TABLE

	Played	Won	Drawn	Lost	Goals For	Goals Against	Pts.
West Germany	3	2	0	1	6	3	4
Austria	3	2	0	1	3	1	4
Algeria	3	2	0	1	5	5	4
Chile	3	0	0	3	3	8	0

GROUP THREE

Belgium	1	Argentina	0
Hungary	10	El Salvador	1
Argentina	4	Hungary	1
Belgium	1	El Salvador	0
Belgium	1	Hungary	1
Argentina	2	El Salvador	0

FINAL TABLE

	Played	Won	Drawn	Lost	Goals For	Goals Against	Pts.
Belgium	3	2	1	0	3	1	5
Argentina	3	2	0	1	6	2	4
Hungary	3	1	1	1	12	6	3
El Salvador	3	0	0	3	1	13	0

GROUP FOUR

England	3	France	1
Czechoslovakia	1	Kuwait	1
England	2	Czechoslovakia	0
France	4	Kuwait	1
Czechoslovakia	1	France	1
England	1	Kuwait	0

FINAL TABLE

	Played	Won	Drawn	Lost	Goals For	Goals Against	Pts.
England	3	3	0	0	6	1	6
France	3	1	1	1	6	5	3
Czecho-slovakia	3	0	2	1	2	4	2
Kuwait	3	0	1	2	2	6	1

GROUP FIVE

Honduras	1	Spain	1
Northern Ireland	0	Yugoslavia	0
Spain	2	Yugoslavia	1
Honduras	1	Northern Ireland	1
Yugoslavia	1	Honduras	0
Northern Ireland	1	Spain	0

FINAL TABLE

	Played	Won	Drawn	Lost	Goals For	Goals Against	Pts.
Northern Ireland	3	1	2	0	2	1	4
Spain	3	1	1	1	3	3	3
Yugoslavia	3	1	1	1	2	2	3
Honduras	3	0	2	1	2	3	2

GROUP SIX

Brazil	2	Soviet Union	1
Scotland	5	New Zealand	2
Brazil	4	Scotland	1
Soviet Union	3	New Zealand	0
Scotland	2	Soviet Union	2
Brazil	4	New Zealand	0

FINAL TABLE

	Played	Won	Drawn	Lost	Goals For	Goals Against	Pts.
Brazil	3	3	0	0	10	2	6
Soviet Union	3	1	1	1	6	4	3
Scotland	3	1	1	1	8	8	3
New Zealand	3	0	0	3	2	12	0

GROUP A

Poland	3	Belgium	0
Soviet Union	1	Belgium	0
Poland	0	Soviet Union	0

FINAL TABLE

	Played	Won	Drawn	Lost	Goals For	Goals Against	Pts.
Poland	2	1	1	0	3	0	3
Soviet Union	2	1	1	0	1	0	3
Belgium	2	0	0	2	0	4	0

GROUP B

England	0	West Germany	0
West Germany	2	Spain	1
England	0	Spain	0

FINAL TABLE

	Played	Won	Drawn	Lost	Goals For	Goals Against	Pts.
West Germany	2	1	1	0	2	1	3
England	2	0	2	0	0	0	2
Spain	2	0	1	1	1	2	1

GROUP C

Italy	2	Argentina	1
Brazil	3	Argentina	1
Italy	3	Brazil	2

FINAL TABLE

	Played	Won	Drawn	Lost	Goals For	Goals Against	Pts.
Italy	2	2	0	0	5	3	4
Brazil	2	1	0	1	5	4	2
Argentina	2	0	0	2	2	5	0

GROUP D

France	1	Austria	0
Austria	2	Northern Ireland	2
France	4	Northern Ireland	1

FINAL TABLE

	Played	Won	Drawn	Lost	Goals For	Goals Against	Pts.
France	2	2	0	0	5	1	4
Austria	2	0	1	1	2	3	1
Northern Ireland	2	0	1	1	3	6	1

SEMIFINALS

Italy	2	Poland	0
West Germany	3	France	3
		(5–4 on penalties)	

THIRD-PLACE PLAY-OFF

Poland	3	France	2

FINAL

Italy	3	West Germany 1

Top goal-scorers: 6 Rossi (Italy); 5 Rummenigge (West Germany); 4 Boniek (Poland); 4 Zico (Brazil).
Fastest goal: 27 seconds, Robson (England vs. France).
Most goals scored: 16 France.
Total goals scored: 146 (average 2.81 per game).
Total attendance: 1,766,277 (average 33,967 per game).
Final attendance: 90,000.

MEXICO 1986

Colombia was chosen as the original host for the 13th World Cup but was forced to withdraw, as the facilities were not considered sufficient to stage a 24-team event.

Brazil, Mexico, and the United States all applied for the right to host the tournament and surprisingly, the vote went to Mexico. A terrible earthquake a year before the finals had devastated Mexico City and nearly caused a second relocation, but the tournament went ahead as planned. The problems of heat and altitude were again a major consideration, but the World Cup was a success despite these problems.

There was yet another change to the format, as the second phase reverted to a knock-out tournament. The top two in each group would qualify, with the four best third-place teams also going through.

The European challenge was led by France, Denmark, West Germany, and Poland. Algeria qualified for the second successive time, and to avoid a repeat of the farce that had seen them lose out four years previously, it had been decided that all the final matches in the groups would be played simultaneously. Brazil and Argentina were the favored teams from South America.

Argentina duly won Group A, drawing 1–1 with the Italians in the big game of the group. Maradona was now at the peak of his career, and from the very first game he proved that he was going to be the most influential player in the tournament. Argentina and Italy qualified, as did Bulgaria, although they still had not won a game in the World Cup finals.

Group B also saw three teams qualify with Mexico,

inspired by their striker Hugo Sanchez, topping the group, to the delight of the home crowd.

Group C saw the Soviet Union and France both finish with five points, but, having beaten Hungary 6–0 in their opening game, the Soviet Union had a superior goal difference. Canada, in their debut, lost all three of their games, but was not disgraced.

Having impressed so many people in 1982, Algeria and Northern Ireland were hoping to build on their previous World Cup successes. However, both were outclassed by Brazil and Spain in a group where third-place teams failed to qualify. Northern Ireland's game against Brazil marked the 41st birthday of their goalkeeper Pat Jennings, and his 119th and last international appearance. As if in tribute, the Brazilians gave their best performance and scored three fabulous goals, presenting him with a signed match ball after the game out of respect for a marvelous career.

With West Germany, Denmark, Scotland, and Uruguay drawn together, Group E earned its nickname, "the group of death." Denmark was in devastating form, winning all three games, including a 6–1 annihilation of Uruguay. Denmark and West Germany qualified, leaving Uruguay and Scotland to play for third place. Scotland needed to win, whereas Uruguay required only a draw to keep their slim hopes of qualifying alive. They hardly improved their chances when, in the first minute, Batista was sent off, but Scotland failed to capitalize on their numerical advantage and a bad-tempered match ended in a draw—good enough for Uruguay.

The teams in Group F had to contend with intense heat and humidity. After a poor start, losing to Portugal and managing only a draw against Morocco, England made several important changes that suddenly transformed them into a team of confidence and enthusiasm.

Though England had been on the brink of an early exit, Gary Lineker scored three goals to beat Poland and take them through to the second phase. Morocco finished at the top of the group with a stunning 3–1 victory over Portugal and became the first African team to qualify for the second round.

The second round got under way in front of more than 100,000 Mexican fans as the hosts took on Bulgaria, who never had a chance to score their first-ever World Cup win as first Negrete, with a spectacular overhead kick, then Servin completed the Mexican victory.

On the same day, Belgium, who had struggled to qualify, faced the Soviet Union in Leon. In a thrilling end-to-end game, Igor Belanov scored a hat trick, but it was not enough, as Belgium won the game 4–3.

The South American favorites advanced further. Poland gave Brazil a few early scares, but once they got into their rhythm there was no stopping the irresistible skills of the Brazilians, as they paced themselves to a 4–0 win. Argentina expected a tough game against their close rival Uruguay. Maradona created plenty of opportunities, but none were converted, and he also had a 30-yard free kick rebound off the crossbar. Pasculli scored for Argentina just before halftime, and although there were no further goals, Argentina was dominant and good for their win.

Italy was no longer the force they had been, and they met a French team approaching their peak. Platini was the driving force behind the team, with able support from Giresse and Tigana in midfield. Platini scored the first and Stopyra the second as Italy, without Rossi, was unable to offer much threat in attack.

West Germany continued to struggle, and it was left to a last-minute free kick from Matthaus to break the Moroccans. England, on the other hand, was visibly growing in confidence, and Lineker notched two more goals in his country's 3–0 win over Paraguay—but only after Shilton, the English goalkeeper, had made two world-class saves early on.

The real surprise of the round was Denmark's defeat at the hands of the Spanish. Denmark had been the revelation of the tournament, and everything seemed to be going well when they took the lead in the 33d minute. Then a terrible error by Olsen allowed Butragueno to equalize for Spain just before halftime. The second half was all Spain and in particular Butragueno, who scored three more as Spain waltzed past the bewildered Danes, 5–1.

In the first of the quarterfinals, France met Brazil in Guadalajara. Careca opened the scoring for Brazil and Muller came close to making it two, his shot hitting the post. It was a stern test for France, but Platini equalized just before halftime. In the second half, Zico, the hero of Brazilian football, was brought on and immediately had the chance to score from a penalty. His kick was saved, and with no further goals in extra time, the game went to a penalty shoot-out. Socrates missed and so did Platini, but Luis Fernandez finally put France into the semifinals.

In the worst of the quarterfinals, West Germany and Mexico battled out a goalless draw and another penalty shoot-out was required. Mexico managed to score only once as West Germany went through to join France.

The third quarterfinal had a special significance, as it was the first meeting between England and Argentina since the end of the Falklands war.

Argentina's disciplined defense controlled Lineker in the early stages, and it was the South Americans, and Maradona in particular, who looked the most dangerous. His first goal is probably the most infamous in World Cup history. The ball had been sliced back in the

England area, and as Maradona rose to meet the high ball with his head he clearly fisted the ball into the net past Shilton. Despite protests from the English players, the Tunisian referee awarded the goal—although in the instant it did look like a good goal.

Four minutes later, there was no denying the brilliance of Maradona's second goal. Collecting the ball in his own half, he waltzed past the English defenders for a truly amazing solo goal.

England belatedly started to attack, and Lineker headed his sixth goal of the tournament and just failed to level the score three minutes from time.

In a wide-open game, Spain and Belgium could not separate the 1-1 stalemate, and for the third quarterfinal a penalty shoot-out was needed. Only one miss by Spain was enough to put Belgium through.

The France–West Germany semifinal was a repeat of the 1982 matchup. Thankfully there was no repeat of the dreadful tackle that had injured Battiston but neither was it as good a game as the 1982 vintage. France was curiously restrained, and never really recovered from an 8th-minute free kick by Brehme. France was committed to pushing forward, which allowed Voller to expose the defense and seal the German victory.

In the other semifinal there was no stopping Maradona as he turned on a magnificent solo performance to take Argentina to the finals. He beat two defenders to score his first goal and then left three defenders for dead before slotting the ball past Pfaff in the Belgian goal.

France was left to contest the third-place play-off for the second successive time, overcoming Belgium 4–2.

In a packed Azteca Stadium, Brown opened the scoring for Argentina with a header in the 22d minute. In the second half Maradona found Enrique, who in turn found Valdano, who cooly put Argentina ahead 2–0. The South Americans were coasting and the West Germans looked in disarray, but as ever they rose to the occasion, and with 17 minutes left Rummenigge pulled West Germany a goal back off a corner kick. Eight minutes later, from an almost identical situation, Voller brought the score level. But Maradona was not to be denied his hour of glory. A sweetly timed pass beat the West German offside trap, and Burruchaga raced away to score the winner.

Argentina had demonstrated that they were more than a one-man team, but there was no denying that Maradona was worthy of the title of the world's best player.

GROUP A

Bulgaria	1	Italy	1
Argentina	3	South Korea	1
Argentina	1	Italy	1
Bulgaria	1	South Korea	1
Argentina	2	Bulgaria	0
Italy	3	South Korea	2

FINAL TABLE

	Played	Won	Drawn	Lost	Goals For	Goals Against	Pts.
Argentina	3	2	1	0	6	2	5
Italy	3	1	2	0	5	4	4
Bulgaria	3	0	2	1	2	4	2
South Korea	3	0	1	2	4	7	1

GROUP B

Mexico	2	Belgium	1
Paraguay	1	Iraq	0
Mexico	1	Paraguay	1
Belgium	2	Iraq	1
Belgium	2	Paraguay	2
Mexico	1	Iraq	0

FINAL TABLE

	Played	Won	Drawn	Lost	Goals For	Goals Against	Pts.
Mexico	3	2	1	0	4	2	5
Paraguay	3	1	2	0	4	3	4
Belgium	3	1	1	1	5	5	3
Iraq	3	0	0	3	1	4	0

GROUP C

France	1	Canada	0
Soviet Union	6	Hungary	0
France	1	Soviet Union	1
Hungary	2	Canada	0
France	3	Hungary	0
Soviet Union	2	Canada	0

FINAL TABLE

	Played	Won	Drawn	Lost	Goals For	Goals Against	Pts.
Soviet Union	3	2	1	0	9	1	5
France	3	2	1	0	5	1	5
Hungary	3	1	0	2	2	9	2
Canada	3	0	0	3	0	5	0

GROUP D

Brazil	1	Spain	0
Algeria	1	Northern Ireland	1
Brazil	1	Algeria	0
Spain	2	Northern Ireland	1
Brazil	3	Northern Ireland	0
Spain	3	Algeria	0

FINAL TABLE

	Played	Won	Drawn	Lost	Goals For	Goals Against	Pts.
Brazil	3	3	0	0	5	0	6
Spain	3	2	0	1	5	2	4
Northern Ireland	3	0	1	2	2	6	1
Algeria	3	0	1	2	1	5	1

GROUP E

West Germany	1	Uruguay	1
Denmark	1	Scotland	0
West Germany	2	Scotland	1
Denmark	6	Uruguay	1
Denmark	2	West Germany	0
Scotland	0	Uruguay	0

FINAL TABLE

	Played	Won	Draws	Lost	Goals For	Goals Against	Pts.
Denmark	3	3	0	0	9	1	6
West Germany	3	1	1	1	3	4	3
Uruguay	3	0	2	1	2	7	2
Scotland	3	0	1	2	1	3	1

GROUP F

Morocco	0	Poland	0
Portugal	1	England	0
England	0	Morocco	0
Poland	1	Portugal	0
England	3	Poland	0
Morocco	3	Portugal	1

FINAL TABLE

	Played	Won	Drawn	Lost	Goals For	Goals Against	Pts.
Morocco	3	1	2	0	3	1	4
England	3	1	1	1	3	1	3
Poland	3	1	1	1	1	3	3
Portugal	3	1	0	2	2	4	2

SECOND ROUND

Mexico	2	Bulgaria	0
Belgium	4	Soviet Union	3
Brazil	4	Poland	0
Argentina	1	Uruguay	0
France	2	Italy	0
West Germany	1	Morocco	0
England	3	Paraguay	0
Spain	5	Denmark	1

QUARTERFINALS

France	1	Brazil	1 (4–3 on penalties)
West Germany	0	Mexico	0 (4–1 on penalties)
Argentina	2	England	1
Belgium	1	Spain	1 (5–4 on penalties)

SEMIFINALS

| West Germany | 2 | France | 0 |
| Argentina | 2 | Belgium | 0 |

THIRD-PLACE PLAY-OFF

| France | 4 | Belgium | 2 |

FINAL

| Argentina | 3 | West Germany | 2 |

Top goal-scorers: 6 Lineker (England); 5 Butragueno (Spain); 5 Careca (Brazil); 5 Maradona (Argentina).

Fastest goal: 63 seconds, Butragueno (Spain vs. Northern Ireland).

Most goals score: 14 Argentina.

Total goals scored : 132 (average 2.54 per game).

Total attendance: 2,391,000 (average 45,980 per game).

Final attendance: 114,500.

ITALY 1990

Italy was awarded the 1990 World Cup at the FIFA Congress in 1984, becoming, along with Mexico, only the second country to host two tournaments. There was considerable concern over the ambitious program for rebuilding stadiums and new rail and road communications, but with huge investment the magnificent stadiums were finished on time.

The format was the same in the 1986 tournament, with the 24 nations divided into six groups of four. The top two in each group went through to the second round along with the four best third-placed teams.

The host nation was rightly considered one of the favorites to lift the trophy, along with West Germany, Holland, Brazil, and Argentina.

Other nations considered strong contenders, like France and Denmark, failed to make it through the qualifying tournament, although the Republic of Ireland qualified for the first time ever.

Argentina, Brazil, Colombia, and Uruguay represented South America, but it was from here that one of the most outrageous attempts to qualify for the finals took place. Chile needed to beat Brazil to qualify and was losing 1–0 when a flare thrown from the crowd appeared to hit their goalkeeper, Roberto Rojas. He collapsed in distress and was carried from the field by officials. The Chilean players claimed they could not continue the match and refused to play. However, television evidence clearly showed that the flare had not hit Rojas, and the Chilean FA was fined by FIFA for its clumsy attempt at cheating and was banned from the 1994 World Cup.

With the enforced absence of Mexico, for fielding overage players in a youth tournament, the door was open for Costa Rica and the United States to qualify from the Central and North American Group group.

South Korea and the United Arab Emirates qualified from Asia, while Africa was represented by Egypt and Cameroon, who, in their previous appearance in 1982, had remained undefeated.

Cameroon proved to be one of the highlights of a tournament that failed to live up to its promise, and announced their intent in the opening game of the finals. Before a crowd of 73,000 in the magnificent San Siro Stadium in Milan, Cameroon took on the champions, Argentina, and although Cameron finished with only nine men, Oman Biyik scored the only goal of the game just five minutes after his brother, Kana Biyik, had been sent off. After this shocking result, Cameroon went about qualifying for the second round with a 2–1 win against Romania. Their hero was Roger Milla, who had come out of semiretirement for the tournament and, at 38, became the oldest man to score in the World Cup. Despite losing their final game to the Soviet Union, Cameroon finished at the top of their group, with Romania second and the defending champion, Argentina, only qualifying as a best third-place team.

In Group A, Italy was under tremendous pressure to succeed. The Italian league is probably the richest and best-supported in the world, and all Italy now wanted victory for the national team. The last time Italy had won the World Cup, in 1982, they had started cautiously with three draws. This time they won all their opening games against Austria, the United States, and Czechoslovakia, and discovered a player who was to hit a rich vein of scoring form—Salvatore "Toto" Schillaci. In the first game,

Italy was by far the better attacking team, but Austria was proving a stubborn opponent. Schillaci was brought on with only 15 minutes remaining and caused widespread celebration by heading the winning goal. Schillaci scored another against the Czechs, in a game that saw him partnered in attack with Roberto Baggio, the young striker who had cost the Italian club, Juventus, $11.25 million.

In Group C, Brazil also qualified with a perfect record, but this was not a team that could be compared with the Brazil of 1970. The attacking flair had been replaced with a more European-style approach, and although they created plenty of chances, they struggled to convert them into goals.

The surprise of the group was Costa Rica, who beat both Sweden and Scotland to qualify with Brazil and also proved that the gap between the established soccer nations and the newcomers is a diminishing one.

The captain of the victorious West German team of 1974, Franz Beckenbauer was now manager of the national team, captained by the inspirational Lothar Matthaus. In the opening match against Yugoslavia, Matthaus scored two goals, the second a brilliant solo effort in which he ran with the ball from just inside his own half before driving a powerful shot from 25 yards.

Having impressively beaten Yugoslavia 4–1, the West Germans put on another fine display in crushing the United Arab Emirates 5–1. In their final game they came up against the skillful Colombians, who had made a welcome return after 28 years. The South Americans knew a draw would be sufficient to get through to the second phase and proceeded to stunt the flow of the game. This was nearly their undoing, as Littbarski scored for West Germany just before full time, only for Rincon to grab an equalizer in injury time.

In Group E, Spain and Belgium proved too strong for South Korea and Uruguay, which, despite talented individuals like Sosa and Francescoli, was in decline as a force in world soccer. The game between the European teams proved to be one of the most entertaining, with both goalkeepers making fine saves. Spain won the game 2–1, and headed the group. The encounter between South Korea and Uruguay was, on the other hand, a dire confrontation, but victory for the South Americans kept them in the tournament.

The final group promised to be the closest of them all—and so it proved. England tied, 1–1, with the Republic of Ireland in a tight game, but it was somewhat surprising that Egypt, making its first appearance in 56 years, held Holland to the same score. In fact, the Dutch team seemed strangely at odds even with their star players—Gullit, Van Basten, and Rijkaard—and Egypt fully deserved their point with some enterprising play. If proof were needed, here it was: The African teams were threatening the soccer world order.

England and Holland then played out a goalless draw, as did Egypt and the Irish. There was everything to play for going into the final games, and England gained the decisive win over Egypt to take them to the top of the table as the other game also finished as a draw.

Egypt was out but Cameroon was still there to represent Africa, and their fairy tale continued in the second round against Colombia. After a goalless 90 minutes, it was super-sub Roger Milla who scored twice in extra time to take the Africans into the quarterfinals.

Tomas Skuhravy scored three of Czechoslovakia's four goals against Costa Rica, although the result does not do full justice to the game. The Costa Ricans were only trailing 2–1 with 15 minutes to go when they were caught twice as they committed players to attack.

The clash between Argentina and Brazil, countries with a great soccer tradition, was a disappointment. Brazil dominated the game but squandered numerous chances to score. They should have won easily, but it was Maradona who made the most telling move. Having been virtually anonymous for most of the game, he played a delightful ball, while under pressure from Brazilian defenders, to Caniggia, who then cooly took the ball around the goalkeeper, Taffarel. Brazil was out.

The same day, the two heavyweights of European football were battling it out in Milan. Holland was the European champion but had been unimpressive in their first-round games. Twenty minutes into the first half, the game had its first major incident. The Dutchman Rijkaard was booked for a foul on the West German striker Voller, who in turn was booked for complaining, with justification, that Rijkaard had spat at him. Shortly after, the two were involved in another dispute and they were both dismissed. As they left the field, Rijkaard again spat at Voller.

Despite this distasteful episode, the quality of football was very good, with the West Germans creating the better chances. In the second half, Klinsmann gave West Germany the lead, and Brehme extended it with a shot that curled around the defense and into the goal. With only minutes left, Holland was awarded a dubious penalty, but it came too late. West Germany won 2–1, the same score as in the 1974 World Cup final.

The Republic of Ireland was enjoying their first-ever finals, and although they had yet to win a game they were through to the second phase to meet Romania, who had the talented Hagi and Raducioiu on their team.

Neither side scored in 120 minutes of play, and in the dreaded penalty shoot-out Timofte missed his kick for Romania. The Irish had qualified for the last eight without winning a game in normal time.

Italy continued to make significant progress, with their star striker, Schillaci, again breaking the deadlock, this time against Uruguay. Serena scored a second, and the crowd erupted in delight. Italy had won every game, had not conceded a goal, and were looking like worthy favorites.

One of the final two matches of the second round saw Yugoslavia beat Spain, thanks to some excellent finishing by Stojkovic in a tight match that went to extra time.

Extra time was also needed to separate England and Belgium. In a close match, the Belgians hit the post twice, one a tremendous strike from 25 yards by Enzo Scifo, and English striker John Barnes scored only for his effort to be ruled offside. With both sides appearing resigned to a shoot-out, England's Gascoigne attacked and was fouled. He took the free kick himself, and David Platt timed his run to swivel and hit the ball on the volley past the Belgian goalkeeper. It was a great goal, and it came with only seconds left in extra time.

After a shaky start, Argentina was now in the quarter-finals, where they faced the classy Yugoslavians. Apart from his one touch of brilliance against Brazil, Maradona had been a shadow of his former self, and his teammates also compared poorly with their predecessors. Yugoslavia displayed the more aggressive soccer throughout the game and looked the more likely to score, but after 120 minutes another penalty competition was required to decide who would go through to the last four.

Sergio Goycochea, who had come in as a replacement

for Argentina's first-choice goalkeeper, was the South American hero, as they won the penalty competition 3–2.

The Irish, yet to win a game, met Italy, who had won all their games, and although Schillaci (who else?) scored the decisive goal for Italy, the Irish put up their best performance of the finals and played with the defiance and commitment that had endeared them to the watching millions.

West Germany rediscovered some of their earlier form and played some fine attacking football. They took the lead when their striker Klinsmann was fouled in the penalty area. Matthaus scored from the spot, but further pressure was well-defended by the Czechs, who had chances to equalize themselves, but could not do so.

The fourth quarterfinal was the best match of the tournament, as Cameroon came within 10 minutes of reaching the last four. This prospect seemed miles away when David Platt gave England the best possible start by heading them into the lead after 26 minutes. But Cameroon had already sent out warning signals, and scored from the penalty spot when Milla had been fouled in the penalty area.

Four minutes later, Milla was causing havoc again, playing a neat one-two with Ekeke, who slotted the ball past Shilton, the English goalkeeper. Cameroon was now in control and looking good for a place in the semifinals, but England, to their credit, reorganized themselves and started to push forward again. A rash challenge on Lineker resulted in a penalty for England nine minutes from time, which Lineker himself converted.

England had come close to elimination, but in the first half of extra time they clinched their place when Lineker was again brought down in the penalty area and again converted his penalty kick. Cameroon had brought a fresh and uninhibited approach to the finals, and their progress had been a true reflection of their ability. They had made England struggle, but the Europeans now had a date with their old foe West Germany.

The first semifinal, however, pitted the hosts against Argentina. Italy started well and went into the lead after 17 minutes when Schillaci scored his fifth goal of the tournament. But with the weight of expectation on them, Italy began to show signs of nerves. They decided to defend their lead, and although they were normally solid in defense, the Argentinians took control of the game and scored a deserved equalizer through Caniggia. The game went into extra time, which produced some unsavory arguing from the Argentinians when Giusti was sent off, but another penalty shoot-out beckoned inexorably.

Both teams scored from their first three kicks, but then Argentinian goalkeeper Goycochea once again demonstrated his amazing skill, saving on Donadoni and Serena. The unthinkable had happened. Italy was out despite having played some of the most attractive and attacking football in the competition.

The West Germans were strong pre-match favorites to join Argentina in the final, but rather than adopt a cagey approach, England was on the offensive from the kick-off and came close to scoring. As it was, West Germany scored a lucky goal that deflected off an English defender over the goalkeeper, Shilton, but England rallied and Lineker equalized with a great strike from a difficult position with two defenders very close. This game also went to penalties. Matthaus converted his, as did Lineker, Beardsley, and Gascoigne for England, to no avail. Pearce and Waddle missed for England, and Matthaus, the German captain, delayed his celebrations to sympathize with the English players.

Both semifinals had been decided on penalties, which had proved a grossly unfair way to decide a match.

The third-place play-off, normally a rather muted occasion, this time produced a match of quality and excitement. Baggio put the Italians ahead, but Platt equalized with a great header nine minutes from time. However, it was appropriate that Schillaci should have the last word. With only five minutes to go he was brought down in the penalty area and converted the kick himself to become the leading scorer in the tournament.

West Germany was expected to win the final with ease. With Italy, they had been the best team in the tournament, and Matthaus had proved to be the world's best player. But just when everyone wanted to see the West Germans put on an exhibition, their form deserted them, and we witnessed the worst final in history.

The West Germans committed themselves to attack but could not convert their chances. This set the standard for the whole game, as Argentina seemed prepared to wait and take their chances in a penalty competition, relying on their outstanding goalkeeper.

Both teams were guilty of playacting. In the 68th minute, the German striker Klinsmann looked as though he had been hit by a train when he was tackled by Monzon, a ruse that succeeded in presenting the Argentinian with the unhappy distinction of becoming the first player to be sent off in a final.

With only five minutes to go, the referee awarded West Germany a penalty after Voller had been fouled in the area. The Argentinian players were furious, as he had turned down a similar-looking offense only minutes earlier. However, Brehme cooly slotted the ball home, even though Goycochea made a valiant attempt and was only inches away from saving it.

The game deteriorated badly in the last few minutes. Kohler, the German defender, appeared to be wasting time and collapsed as if he had been poleaxed when Dezotti tried to retrieve the ball off him. Dezotti was also sent off by the referee as several Argentinian players jostled the official in a disgraceful show.

It was a shame that the West Germans had not beaten Argentina in the style they had shown earlier in the tournament. The final did nothing for the game, and what is the ultimate accolade for any footballer or fan was tarnished by this episode.

GROUP A

Italy	1	Austria	0
Czechoslovakia	5	United States	1
Italy	1	United States	0
Czechoslovakia	1	Austria	0
Italy	2	Czechoslovakia	0
Austria	2	United States	1

FINAL TABLE

	Played	Won	Drawn	Lost	Goals For	Goals Against	Pts.
Italy	3	3	0	0	4	0	6
Czecho-slovakia	3	2	0	1	6	3	4
Austria	3	1	0	2	2	3	2
United States	3	0	0	3	2	8	0

All eyes will be on the United States team as they take on the rest of the world in soccer's greatest showcase. Coach Bora Milutinovic will have prepared his team well. He is experienced at developing good team spirit and commitment from his players. (Photos courtesy of Allsport)

Roy Wegerle, one of the Europe-based players, in action. His international experience and great individual skill will be essential for his United States team.
(Photo courtesy of Allsport)

The unmistakable sight of Colombian playmaker and 1993 South American Footballer of the Year, Carlos Valderrama. His touch and vision could help his team go far.
(Photo courtesy of Allsport)

Heading for America. Ciriaco Sforza demonstrates his commitment and ball-winning ability. He is a key figure in the Swiss midfield.
(Photo courtesy of Allsport)

Brazilian fans will be hoping for more spectacular goals and less controversy from the brilliant Farrias Romario.

(Photos courtesy of Allsport)

François Oman-Biyik will once again be spearheading the Cameroon attack. Scorer of the goal that beat Argentina four years ago, here he is in typical committed action against Zimbabwe.

Martin Dahlin is the new star of Swedish football. He is very quick and powerful and a lethal goalscorer.

(Photo courtesy of Allsport)

Although 33, Lothar Matthaus is still the driving force behind the German team. He is an inspirational captain and has won every honor in football.

(Photo courtesy of Allsport)

Andoni Zubizarreta is Spain's most-capped player and is one of the finest goalkeepers in the world.

(Photo courtesy of Allsport)

Gabriel Batistuta is Argentina's leading scorer; he can create goals from nothing despite being heavily marked and, at times, operating as a lone striker.

(Photos courtesy of Allsport)

Argentina is not the team they were in 1978, but Batistuta will be keen to emulate the top striker of the 1978 Cup-winning team—Mario Kempes—seen here tearing into the Dutch defense.

Diego Maradona was the star of the 1986 tournament when his powerful runs destroyed teams almost single-handedly. Then, he was the best footballer in the world and the world was at his feet. But now he may not even play in the finals.

(Photo courtesy of Allsport)

There is a huge weight of expectancy on the shoulders of Roberto Baggio to prove that he is the world's best. His performance will be vital to Italy's progress.

(Photo courtesy of Allsport)

Look out for the colorful Jorge Campos. A brilliant and agile goalkeeper, he may also be seen making daring forays outside his penalty area in support of his defense.

(Photo courtesy of Allsport)

One of the most promising players in England, Roy Keane (left) is a vital cog in the Irish team. His youth, stamina, and tireless running will be essential elements in an aging team.

(Photo courtesy of Allsport)

Enzo Scifo is the creative inspiration behind the Belgian team and can score spectacular goals from long distances.
(Photo courtesy of Allsport)

Ruud Gullit has had a great season in Italy and should be full of confidence and determined to improve on Holland's poor display in 1990. He is quick and very strong in attack. He may not have the speed of Johan Cruyff—seen below in action against West Germany in the 1974 final—but Gullit could prove just as inspirational.
(Photos courtesy of Allsport)

Champions past. Winning the World Cup is the ultimate honor in football. Dino Zoff played a major role in Italy's World Cup–winning team of 1982 and celebrates with the trophy.

England's captain, Bobby Moore, and teammate Jack Charlton set off on a victory lap, cheered by the ecstatic English fans. Now the manager of the Republic of Ireland team, Jack Charlton will be hoping to get his hands on the World Cup trophy as winners this year. Competition will be tough. (Photos courtesy of Allsport)

GROUP B

Cameroon	1	Argentina	0
Romania	2	Soviet Union	0
Argentina	2	Soviet Union	0
Cameroon	2	Romania	1
Soviet Union	4	Cameroon	0
Argentina	1	Romania	1

FINAL TABLE

	Played	Won	Drawn	Lost	Goals For	Goals Against	Pts.
Cameroon	3	2	0	1	3	5	4
Romania	3	1	1	1	4	3	3
Argentina	3	1	1	1	3	2	3
Soviet Union	3	1	0	2	4	4	2

GROUP C

Brazil	2	Sweden	1
Costa Rica	1	Scotland	0
Brazil	1	Costa Rica	0
Scotland	2	Sweden	1
Costa Rica	2	Sweden	1
Brazil	1	Scotland	0

FINAL TABLE

	Played	Won	Drawn	Lost	Goals For	Goals Against	Pts.
Brazil	3	3	0	0	4	1	6
Costa Rica	3	2	0	1	3	2	4
Scotland	3	1	0	2	2	3	2
Sweden	3	0	0	3	3	6	0

GROUP D

Colombia	2	United Arab Emirates	0
West Germany	4	Yugoslavia	1
Yugoslavia	1	Colombia	0
West Germany	5	United Arab Emirates	1
Colombia	1	West Germany	1
Yugoslavia	4	United Arab Emirates	1

FINAL TABLE

	Played	Won	Drawn	Lost	Goals For	Goals Against	Pts.
West Germany	3	2	1	0	10	3	5
Yugoslavia	3	2	0	1	6	5	4
Colombia	3	1	1	1	3	2	3
United ArabEmirates	3	0	0	3	2	11	0

GROUP E

Belgium	2	South Korea	0
Spain	0	Uruguay	0
Spain	3	South Korea	1
Belgium	3	Uruguay	1
Spain	2	Belgium	1
Uruguay	1	South Korea	0

FINAL TABLE

	Played	Won	Drawn	Lost	Goals For	Goals Against	Pts.
Spain	3	2	1	0	5	2	5
Belgium	3	2	0	1	6	3	4
Uruguay	3	1	1	1	2	3	3
South Korea	3	0	0	3	1	6	0

GROUP F

England	1	Republic of Ireland	1
Egypt	1	Holland	1
England	0	Holland	0
Egypt	0	Republic of Ireland	0
England	1	Egypt	0
Holland	1	Republic of Ireland	1

FINAL TABLE

	Played	Won	Drawn	Lost	Goals For	Goals Against	Pts.
England	3	1	2	0	2	1	4
Republic of Ireland	3	0	3	0	2	2	3
Holland	3	0	3	0	2	2	3
Egypt	3	0	2	1	1	2	2

SECOND ROUND

Cameroon	2	Colombia	1
Czechoslovakia	4	Costa Rica	1
Argentina	1	Brazil	0
West Germany	2	Holland	1
Republic of Ireland	0	Romania	0 (5–4 on penalties)
Italy	2	Uruguay	0
Yugoslavia	2	Spain	1
England	1	Belgium	0

QUARTERFINALS

Argentina	0	Yugoslavia	0 (3–2 on penalties)
Italy	1	Republic of Ireland	0
West Germany	1	Czechoslovakia	0
England	3	Cameroon	2

SEMIFINALS

Argentina	1	Italy	1 (4–3 on penalties)
West Germany	1	England	1 (4–3 on penalties)

THIRD-PLACE PLAY-OFF

Italy	2	England	1

FINAL

West Germany	1	Argentina	0

Top goal-scorers: 6 Schillaci (Italy); 5 Skuhravy (Czechoslovakia); 4 Lineker (England); 4 Matthaus (West Germany); 4 Michel (Spain); 4 Milla (Cameroon).

Fastest goal: 4 minutes, Susic (Yugoslavia vs. United Arab Emirates).

Most goals scored: 15 West Germany.

Total goals scored: 150 (average 2.21 per game).

Total attendance: 2,515,000 (average 48,365 per game).

Final attendance: 73,603.

THE VENUES

The selection of nine World Cup venues from the original 32 cities that had expressed interest in hosting the 1994 World Cup games took two years to complete. It all started in January 1990, when cities as diverse as Honolulu and Boston expressed interest in submitting their applications to host the games. World Cup USA personnel visited each city, and by May 1, 1991, the closing date for filing bids, the organizing committee had received an amazing 27 complete, documented bids.

Each bid committee made a series of presentations in Los Angeles May 20–23, 1991, to the World Cup organizers, who then spent the summer evaluating each bid. By October of the same year, 19 applicants were selected as "priority venues."

A technical group of FIFA experts then inspected the 19 priority venue cities to assess physical locality, support from the local community, and the technical merits of the stadiums.

The nine successful bids were decided on March 23, 1992; bid committees became host committees and set about organizing and promoting activities around their World Cup games.

BOSTON

Foxboro Stadium
   Built: 1970.
   Location: Midway between Boston and Providence.
   Capacity: 61,000.
   Size: 105 x 68m.
   World Cup schedule: First round, June 21, 23, 25, 30;
      Second round, July 5; Quarterfinal, July 9.

The Massachusetts area was responsible for many of U.S. soccer's great teams and players in its early days, the Portuguese influence in the area no doubt helping.

Foxboro Stadium, home of the New England Patriots, has hosted the U.S. national team in the World Series/U.S. Cup. In 1991, the game between the U.S. and Ireland drew a crowd of 54,743, and the two U.S. Cup matches in 1992 drew a combined audience of 75,000. In the U.S. Cup '93, the United States beat England for the first time in 43 years here.

Boston is famed for its importance in the American Revolution. Its banking and financial centers are of major importance to New England's economy.

CHICAGO

Soldier Field
   Built: 1922.
   Location: Shores of Lake Michigan.
   Capacity: 66,814.
   Size: 105 x 68m.
   World Cup schedule: First round, June 17, 21, 26, 27;
      Second round, July 2.

Chicago is home to the governing body of U.S. soccer and has produced many national U.S. champions, most recently the AAC Eagles, who captured the U.S. Open Cup in 1990. The Chicago Sting were champions of the North American Soccer League in 1991.

Soldier Field is scheduled to stage the 1994 World Cup opening ceremony and Germany's first-round matches. It is famous for its monumental exterior and the classical colonnades lining each side.

Built in 1924, it was originally a U-shaped arena, but a new stand was added to create an enclosure when the Chicago Bears made it their home in 1971. In 1988 its artificial surface was replaced with real turf.

Chicago is the third-largest city in the United States and one of the wealthiest in the Midwest. It is home to more than 80 ethnic communities. Cultural instititutions include the Museum of Science and Industry, and the Field Museum of Natural History. Chicago also boasts three of the tallest man-made structures in the world: the Sears Tower, the Amoco Building, and the John Hancock Building.

DALLAS

Cotton Bowl
  Built: 1930.
  Location: Center of the historic Fair Park, a 273-acre
        site containing museums, a planetarium, aquarium,
        and Ferris wheel.
  Capacity: 72,000.
  Size: 105 x 68m.
  World Cup schedule: First round, June 17, 21, 27, 30;
        Second round, July 3; Quarterfinal, July 9.

Long a hotbed of youth soccer, Dallas is the home of the American Airlines Dallas Cup, one of the most prestigious youth soccer events in the world. The Cotton Bowl hosted the 1993 CONCACAF Gold Cup tournament won by Mexico. The stadium used to be the home of the Dallas Cowboys until 1970. The artificial surface has recently been replaced by grass.

Located in the heart of northern Texas, Dallas is famed for its production of oil and natural gas, but has a broad economic base producing crops and livestock. Dallas also houses one of the largest inland cotton markets and has a strong financial sector.

DETROIT

Pontiac Silverdome
    Built: 1975.
    Location: 18 miles from Detroit.
    Capacity: 76,000.
    Size: 103 x 66m.
    World Cup schedule: First round, June 18, 22, 24, 28.

The United States will play their opening game on June 18 in the Pontiac Silverdome, Detroit—the first World Cup match to be played indoors.

Capable of accommodating every citizen in Pontiac, this is the largest covered arena in the world and the home of the Detroit Lions. The teams will play in a constant temperature of 72°F. To comply with FIFA's rules, the artificial surface had to be replaced with grass. Houston, one of the original contenders, and New Orleans, the only other indoor alternative, shared with Detroit the cost of an $85,000 experiment that proved to be a great success.

Roger Faulkner, the Michigan chairman, who was born in England, insisted that a field could be sown outside, transported indoors, and withstand the harsh playing conditions; the grass could even be designed to a specific texture.

After visiting the stadium in which Madonna and the Rolling Stones have appeared, Guido Tognoni, FIFA's press officer, described it as "a five-star stadium, a special place."

LOS ANGELES

Rose Bowl
    Built: 1922
    Location: Pasadena (seven miles from L.A.).
    Capacity: 102,083.
    Size: 105 x 68m.
    World Cup schedule: First round, June 18, 19, 22, 26;
        Second round, July 3; Semifinal, July 13; Third-
        place play-off, July 16; Final, July 17.

L.A.'s success in soccer dates back to 1958, when the Los Angeles Kickers won the U.S. Open Cup. It has hosted many international events, most notably the 1984 Olympic soccer tournament, where attendance remains the highest of any sport in any Olympics (Brazil versus France attracted 101,799). Johann Cruyff and George Best both played for the L.A. Aztecs.

The Rose Bowl has hosted five Super Bowls.

Famous for its importance in the film industry, Los Angeles is one of the three great industrial cities of the United States. Rail, road, and air communications are superb, and the city has 46 miles of waterfront.

• • •

NEW YORK/NEW JERSEY

Giants Stadium
   Built: 1976.
   Location: East Rutherford, New Jersey.
   Capacity: 76,891.
   Size: 103 x 66m.
   World Cup schedule: First round, June 18, 23, 25, 28;
       Second round, July 5; Quarterfinal, July 10;
       Semifinal, July 13.

This whole area is steeped in sports. Giants Stadium forms part of the Meadowlands Sports Complex (along with Brendan Byrne Arena and Meadowlands Racetrack).

Giants Stadium is home to the New York Giants and the New York Jets during the American football season, and hosts concerts and shows out-of-season.

From 1977 to 1984 the stadium was home to the Cosmos, who played before some of the largest crowds in U.S. soccer history (N.Y. Cosmos versus Argentina, 70,134; Pele's farewell, 76,891). This is not surprising, as the Cosmos team included some of the most famous soccer players in history: Pele, Beckenbauer, Carlos Alberto, and Neeskens all wore the Cosmos stripes.

New York is the largest city in the United States. Within the five boroughs—Manhattan, Brooklyn, the Bronx, Queens, and Staten Island—there is an exciting mix of cultures, attractions, restaurants, shops, and nightlife.

ORLANDO

Citrus Bowl
   Built: 1976.
   Location: One mile west of downtown Orlando.

Capacity: 70,188.
Size: 105 x 68m.
World Cup schedule: First round, June 19, 24, 25, 29;
        Second round, July 4.

This area has been designated by U.S. Soccer as a national training center for the U.S. national team.

The Citrus Bowl was the venue for the United States' games against Australia in 1992 and Russia in 1993.

Orlando is one of the country's fastest-growing areas. It boasts the world's most popular tourist attraction, DisneyWorld, as well as Sea World and Universal Studios.

It boasts the United States' second largest international airport and welcomes millions of tourists every year who come to enjoy Florida's perfect climate and beautiful scenery.

SAN FRANCISCO

Stanford Stadium
    Built: 1921.
    Location: Palo Alto, 27 miles south of San Francisco.
    Capacity: 86,019.
    Size: 105 x 68m.
    World Cup schedule: First round, June 20, 24, 26, 28;
        Second round, July 4; Quarterfinal, July 10.

In 1990 Stanford Stadium hosted the match between the U.S. and the Soviet Union, which attracted a crowd of 61,000. It was also a venue for soccer at the 1984 Olympics. The San Francisco Bay area has some 200,000 registered youth players.

WASHINGTON, D.C.

RFK Stadium
   Built: 1961.
   Location: Twenty blocks east of the U.S. Capitol.
   Capacity: 56,500.
   Size: 105 x 68m.
   World Cup schedule: First round, June 19, 20, 28, 29;
       Second round, July 2.

Soccer in Washington dates back to the turn of the century—club teams were formed by staff at the various embassies.

RFK was the home of the Washington Diplomats, for whom the great Johann Cruyff played. The 1980 NASL Soccer Bowl between the Cosmos and Fort Lauderdale was played here, with an attendance of 50,768.

THE TEAMS

 **GROUP A**

UNITED STATES, COLOMBIA, ROMANIA, SWITZERLAND

It will not be easy for the United States to maintain the tradition of the host nation advancing to the second round, and it is imperative that they win their opening game against Switzerland, who may be overawed by the occasion. Colombia looks to be the strongest team and will have benefited from both their experience in the 1990 World Cup finals and an impressive qualification. For Romania, two matches in Los Angeles separated by a match against the Swiss in Detroit may not be ideal, and they could end up in a decider against the hosts at the Rose Bowl.

GROUP A FIXTURES

United States vs. Switzerland	June 18 (Detroit)
Colombia vs. Romania	June 18 (Los Angeles)
United States vs. Colombia	June 22 (Los Angeles)
Switzerland vs. Romania	June 22 (Detroit)
United States vs. Romania	June 26 (Los Angeles)
Switzerland vs. Colombia	June 26 (San Francisco)

UNITED STATES

Governing body: United States Soccer Federation.
Founded: 1913.
Affiliated to FIFA: 1913.
National colors: White shirts, blue shorts, white socks
(all with red, white, and blue piping).
Manager/Coach: Bora Milutinovic.

When the United States beat England 1–0 in the 1950
World Cup finals, the victory became a stunning part of
sporting legend. Walter Bahr, who assisted in the goal,
then said: "Another 50 years and we'll really be famous."

Well, 44 years on, the United States has failed to live
up to this promise or achievement, but all that may be
rectified this year. The rest of the world may not be giving
the home nation much of a chance of progressing through
the tournament, but the team has very different ideas.

Much of the confidence is based around the U.S.
coach, Bora Milutinovic. Born a Serb in 1944, he played
for Partizan Belgrade in the 1960s before moving on to
play in France with Nice and Monaco. He later moved to
the Mexican club Universidad Nacional before retiring
from playing in 1975. On his travels he has picked up
Spanish, Italian, French, and English, but whatever language he works in, it does the trick: He got Mexico to
the quarterfinals in 1986, and Costa Rica past Scotland
and Sweden to the second round of Italia 1990.

In March 1991 he took on the American team. And
he has started to live up to his "Miracle Man" nickname.
The players swear by him; they say he simplifies the game
instead of making it complex. He gives then confidence
to do things other coaches might stop them from doing.
He engenders the teamwork ethic that helps compensate
for deficiencies his team may have in individual skill.

But for Milutinovic it is not a matter, as it is for other national managers, of choosing a squad from the best league players, for at the moment there is no league. His problem has been that he never has his best players. John Harkes and Roy Wegerle are in England's Premier league; Tab Ramos plays in Spain; Ernie Stewart is in Holland; and Eric Wynalda and Thomas Dooley both play in the Bundesliga in Germany. Milutinovic has said, "The main purpose of USA '94 is that soccer should grow in America, and a pro league be established. If the league doesn't come after 1994, then we will have only done half the job."

The NASL may have folded in 1985, but among the American squad you will find many native-born players who grew up admiring a particular team. For John Harkes from New Jersey, it was the Cosmos—as a kid he had tail-gate parties in the parking lot before the games. For Eric Wynalda, it was Johann Cruyff and the Los Angeles Aztecs, and for Jeff Agoos it was the Dallas Raiders.

So the idea that these Americans do not know about soccer is untrue. It may not be in their blood, but more kids play it now than any other sport but basketball, and more Division One colleges have soccer programs than American football programs. And American women, who represent more than a third of the 16 million players in the country, have achieved a notable and equally unacclaimed feat. They are the current world champions.

Eric Wynalda said: "The American team can play with anybody. They can call us a green-card team, they can call us whatever they want, that's fine. We've got a great coach, we've got some great players, so let's just see what happens."

They must make the most of the benefits and privileges that come with being the host nation. The U.S. is not to be underestimated. They play as a team, as they proved when beating England in Boston.

And although plain reading of the record for the U.S. in 1993 appears unimpressive—11 wins, 12 losses, and 1 draw—this was achieved effectively with two teams. First there is the team that is under full-time contract at the Federation's training ground at Mission Viejo, California. Then there is the team that plays when Milutinovic can get his overseas players released by their clubs. And they have collected several notable scalps in the form of Ireland, England, and Portugal, and have drawn with Italy.

The American team will have the benefit of having trained and played together for over a year, and Milutinovic will have molded them into a tight, cohesive team. They also possess great team spirit and unbounding enthusiasm to do well.

Route to the Finals
Qualified by right as hosts

World Cup History
Soccer in America has a long tradition. The first club was formed in 1862 in Boston, and it is interesting that this predates any club outside of England. However, once American football had been adopted and started to grow in popularity, soccer became more of a pastime of the numerous ethnic communities.

A national team took part in the 1924 and 1928 Olympic Games; and in the very first World Cup held in Uruguay, the United States beat Belgium and Paraguay to qualify for the semifinals. In a tough encounter, they lost 6–1 to Argentina.

Four years later they made the long trip to Italy, only to return shortly after having lost their first game. But this was compensated for in the 1950 World Cup in Brazil. This time, the team was composed almost entirely of American-born players, and after an unlucky defeat against Spain, they produced the single greatest shock in the history of the World Cup. In Belo Horizonte, Joe Gaetjens scored a goal that humbled the mighty English team.

It was not until 1990 that the United States managed to qualify for the finals again. Despite strong team spirit, the Americans were brought down to earth by Czechoslovakia but showed great resolve as they tightened up their game for the match against Italy. They lost, 1–0, but came out of the game and the tournament with credit and respectability.

Finals appearances: 4 (1930, 1934, 1950, 1990).
Biggest win: 3–0 vs. Belgium (1930); 3–0 vs. Paraguay (1930).
Biggest defeat: 1–7 vs. Italy (1934).
Leading scorer: Bert Patenaude (3 goals).

RECORD

Played	Won	Drawn	Lost	Goals For	Goals Against
10	3	0	7	14	29

1930 Semifinalists
Group Four: 3–0 vs. Belgium, 3–0 vs. Paraguay; Semifinal: 1–6 vs. Argentina.

1934 Eliminated first round
First round: 1–7 vs. Italy.

1950 Eliminated first round
Group Two: 1–3 vs. Spain, 1–0 vs. England, 2–5 vs. Chile.

1990 Eliminated first round
Group A: 1–5 vs. Czechoslovakia, 0–1 vs. Italy, 1–2 vs. Austria.

COLOMBIA

Governing body: *Federacion Colombiana de Futbol.*
Founded: 1924.
Affiliated to FIFA: 1936.
National colors: Yellow shirts, blue shorts, red socks.
Manager/Coach: Francisco Maturana.

Colombia was responsible for perhaps the biggest shock of the World Cup qualifiers when they beat Argentina, the reigning South American champions, at the River Plata Stadium in Buenos Aires. The victory itself was not surprising—Colombia had already beaten Argentina 2–1 at home in an earlier qualification game—it was the emphatic nature and margin of victory, 5–0, that heralded Colombia as the most improved team of the year and a major force in world soccer.

Colombia's first win, in Barranquilla, ended Argentina's longest-ever unbeaten run of 31 internationals, and the second defeat was Argentina's worst in 83 years.

These performances crowned a great year for coach Francisco Maturana and took Colombia's unbeaten record to 20 games. The general opinion was that they were the best team in the 1993 South American Championship held in Ecuador, where they finished third, and after their unbeaten World Cup qualifying record, Colombia can look forward to putting up a bold show in the finals.

Colombian soccer has been plagued with controversy throughout the years. Stories of money-laundering and of referees being bribed and assassinated by drug barons have given the South Americans a bad name in world soccer but, despite all this, they appear to be on the verge of achieving great success—success that has taken its time in coming.

After years of importing talent from around the world, the Colombian league took control of the number of foreign players in the 1970s, and local talent began to develop. The fortunes of the national team also improved throughout the 1980s with good performances in the South American Championship and in the qualifications for the 1990 World Cup. They certainly made their mark on the tournament, and their attractive style of soccer won them many admirers, but they struggled to find consistency. Fortunately they remained true to their values of how the game should be played and are now playing with skill and confidence. In their last two qualifying games for the 1994 tournament, the goals started to flow, and many neutrals hope that this continues into the World Cup.

A team with as much flair as their rival Brazil, Colombia bases their success on a typically South American attacking game. They retain possession in defense, play the ball through midfield with short, close passing, and quicken the tempo as they hit the opposition's penalty area. Players are constantly running into space and creating plenty of attacking options. This open and attractive style of play should pull in the crowds, and hot, humid conditions will surely suit their close-passing game.

Without doubt the most recognizable of the Colombians is the midfield playmaker Carlos Valderrama, who is involved in the buildup behind many of the Colombians' moves, but the player who will make the biggest impression in the finals is likely to be Faustino Asprilla. Not only is he an extremely gifted attacking player, he is also controversial and unpredictable.

Asprilla scored two of the goals against Argentina and assisted in a third, while for his Italian club, Parma, one of his many spectacular goals was the one that ended AC

Milan's 68-match, 21-month unbeaten league run. Asprilla's blistering pace and sensational strikes will make him a handful for any team.

One character who will not be around from the 1990 finals is goalkeeper Rene Higuita. Famed for his forays upfield, often to be found near the halfway line, Higuita recently spent time in jail for allegedly acting as a go-between in a kidnapping.

When Colombia beat Argentina, celebrations across the country lasted for days, with reports of up to 100 deaths due to the mass hysteria. One fears what might happen were they to win the World Cup itself.

Route to the Finals

South America: Group A

Colombia	0	Paraguay	0
Colombia	1	Peru	0
Colombia	2	Argentina	1
Colombia	1	Paraguay	1
Colombia	4	Peru	0
Colombia	5	Argentina	0

Played	Won	Drawn	Lost	Goals For	Goals Against	Pts.
6	4	2	0	13	2	10

Colombia won Group A.

World Cup History

Colombia made their World Cup finals debut in 1962, and after a scrappy defeat against Uruguay they pulled off the surprise of the tournament with a 4–4 draw against the Soviet Union. They had been trailing 4–1 with only 35 minutes of the game remaining when they decided to throw everything into the attack. After such a tremendous fight back, the Colombians were understandably exhausted and couldn't put up such stern opposition to an efficient Yugoslavian side.

Colombia made a welcome return to the World Cup in 1990 with a victory against the United Arab Emirates, their first in the finals. A loss to Yugoslavia meant that a draw was needed against West Germany to see them through to the second round. This led to Colombia displaying the less attractive aspects of South American soccer—time-wasting—that were very nearly their undoing, as Littbarski scored in the 89th minute for West Germany. Spurred into action, Carlos Valderrama split the German defense with an accurate pass to Rincon, who equalized two minutes into injury time.

The second-round tie against Cameroon belonged to the 38-year-old African Roger Milla, who scored two goals in extra time to see his team through to the quarterfinals.

Finals appearances: 2 (1962, 1990).
Biggest win: 2–0 vs. United Arab Emirates (1990).
Biggest defeat: 0–5 vs. Yugoslavia (1962).
Leading scorer: Bernardo Redin Valverde (2 goals).

RECORD

Played	Won	Drawn	Lost	Goals For	Goals Against
7	1	2	4	9	15

• •

1962   **Eliminated first round**
Group One: 1–2 vs. Uruguay, 4–4 vs. Soviet
Union, 0–5 vs. Yugoslavia.
1990   **Eliminated second round**
Group D: 2–0 vs. United Arab Emirates, 0–1 vs.
Yugoslavia, 1–1 vs. West Germany; Second
round: 1–2 vs. Cameroon.

• •

ROMANIA

Governing body: *Federatia Romana de Fotbal*.
Founded: 1908.
Affiliated to FIFA: 1930.
National colors: Yellow shirts, yellow shorts, yellow socks.
Manager/Coach: Anghel Iordanescu.

Romania came with a late charge to win their final three
games and qualify for the finals. Group Four was one of
the most competitive of the European groups, with four
teams having a realistic chance of taking one of the two
qualification places.

Romania made a bright start, but a defeat against
Belgium and a draw against Czechoslovakia damaged
their chances, particularly as Romania should have won
both games. In the return leg against the newly named
RCS (Representation of Czechs and Slovaks), they suffered an astonishing 2–5 defeat in which the commitment of the players was called into question. Romania's
chances looked slim, but consecutive victories over the

Faroe Isles, fellow finalists Belgium, and Wales booked their passage to the United States.

The appointment of coach Anghel Iordanescu, one of the great names in Romanian football, after the debacle against the RCS was instrumental in Romania's upturn in form, and he now has the task of forming a cohesive squad in time for the finals. He does have a number of players of exceptional ability to choose from, but his problem lies with the fact that the majority of the Romanian players play abroad. As the various seasons in Italy, Germany, and Spain reach their conclusions, Iordanescu will find it difficult to obtain the release of his top players from their clubs for vital friendly matches.

In the late 1980s, a national manager would have had no such problems, as many of Romania's best players played for the state-supported army team, Steaua Bucharest, which also made up much of the national team. Steaua was one of the most successful teams in Europe, winning the European Cup in 1986, but after the Romanian revolution and the 1990 World Cup, many of these players were bought by Italian and Spanish clubs for large fees.

The Romanians always played well as a team, mainly because many of them were teammates at club level as well as at national level. This aspect may not be as evident in this World Cup, but they are still a precise passing team with many talented individuals. Their most outstanding player is Gheorghe Hagi, one of the world's best attacking midfielders. He has exceptional skill and a devastating left-foot shot. He often takes up a deep position where it is difficult for opposing players to pick him up. Hagi is at his most dangerous when running at defenses from these positions or supplying accurate and decisive passes to his forwards.

Florin Raducioiu is an exceptional striker with pace and control. He moved to Italy in 1990 after creating a favorable impression in the 1990 World Cup at the age of 20. Ilie Dumitrescu, another prolific scorer for his club and country, still plays in Romania but is sure to attract a lot of attention with his attacking runs from midfield.

Although they will be short on support, Romania could make the second round.

Route to the Finals

Europe: Group Four

Romania	7	Faroe Islands	0
Romania	5	Wales	1
Romania	0	Belgium	1
Romania	1	RCS	1
Romania	4	Cyprus	1
Romania	2	Cyprus	1
RCS	5	Romania	2
Romania	4	Faroe Islands	0
Romania	2	Belgium	1
Romania	2	Wales	1

Played	Won	Drawn	Lost	Goals For	Goals Against	Pts.
10	7	1	2	29	12	15

Romania won Group Four.

World Cup History

Romania had the distinction of playing in the first World Cup tournament but only made the trip following the insistence of their king—a great fan of football—that Romania take part. He selected the team himself and persuaded their employers to allow them three months' leave to travel to South America. King Carol didn't make a bad job of picking the team, either, as they opened with a 3–1 victory over Peru. It was a tough game and Peru's Mario de la Casas earned the dubious distinction of becoming the first man to be sent off in the World Cup. In their next game they lost to the eventual champion, Uruguay.

Having played in the first three World Cup finals, being eliminated in the first round of each, Romania failed to qualify or did not enter the competition again until 1970. Once more they failed to survive the opening round, although their group contained England and Brazil, who were everyone's favorites to reach the final itself.

They failed to qualify for the next four finals but headed their qualification group in 1990. In the finals, they faced defending champion Argentina, Cameroon, and the Soviet Union in Group B. Victory over Russia and a draw against Argentina was sufficient to get them through to the second phase despite losing to the surprise team of the tournament, Cameroon. In the quarterfinals they faced the Republic of Ireland and were unlucky to lose in a penalty shoot-out.

Finals appearances: 5 (1930, 1934, 1938, 1970, 1990).
Biggest win: 3–1 vs. Peru (1930).
Biggest defeat: 0–4 vs. Uruguay (1930).
Leading scorer: Stefan Dobai (3 goals).

RECORD

Played	Won	Drawn	Lost	Goals For	Goals Against
12	3	2	7	16	20

• •

1930   **Eliminated first round**
Group Three: 3–1 vs. Peru, 0–4 vs. Uruguay.
1934   **Eliminated first round**
First round: 1–2 vs. Czechoslovakia.
1938   **Eliminated first round**
First round: 3–3 vs. Cuba, 1–2 vs. Cuba (replay).
1970   **Eliminated first round**
Group Three: 0–1 vs. England, 2–1 vs.
Czechoslovakia, 2–3 vs. Brazil.
1990   **Eliminated second round**
Group B: 2–0 vs. Soviet Union, 1–2 vs.
Cameroon, 1–1 vs. Argentina; Second round:
0–0 vs. Republic of Ireland (4–5 in penalties).

• •

SWITZERLAND

Governing body: *Schweizerischer Fussballverband.*
Founded: 1895.
Affiliated to FIFA: 1904.
National colors: Red shirts, white shorts, red socks.
Manager/Coach: Roy Hodgson.

Switzerland had not reached the finals of a major competition since the 1966 World Cup finals held in England, but they sealed their qualification for the United States World Cup in some style with a 4–0 win over Estonia in Zurich.

Having made an impressive start to the qualifying stages with wins in their opening two matches, Switzerland's first serious test in Group One came on October 14, 1992, when they traveled to Cagliari to play the group favorite Italy. The result of this match gave a good indication as to how serious the Swiss challenge would be. Results in recent years suggested that they might wilt under the pressure-cooker atmosphere, but in front of a fervent Italian crowd, Switzerland struck twice within the first 20 minutes, and only two late Italian goals in the 83d and 90th minutes denied them a victory.

The tie was an excellent result, and Switzerland proved they were going to be a tough team to beat. They maintained their challenge for qualification with wins over Malta, and a 1–1 draw against Portugal was only a minor setback. The subsequent 1–0 victory over Italy in Bern confirmed them as worthy qualifiers.

When Englishman Roy Hodgson took over as national coach in 1992 (from German Uli Stielike), Switzerland was a talented but inconsistent team. Over the past two to three years they have improved steadily and developed consistency in terms of players and tactics.

The strength of the team is that it is now a settled team, combining youth and experience. Many Swiss believe Hodgson has worked a miracle in guiding the national team to the finals, but what he has achieved is to instill confidence in the team to the extent that the players believe they can win—no mean feat after 28 years of non-qualification for a major finals.

Although they rely on a strong all-around team performance, the Swiss also have several talented players. In Stephane Chapuisat they have a world-class striker with a deadly left foot who plays club soccer for Borussia Dortmund in the German league. He is a prolific goal-scorer for his club and country, but is also adept at providing accurate passes for his tall striking partner, Adrian Knup.

Another key member of the team, Ciriaco Sforza, also plays in the German league. The 24-year-old central midfielder, who joined Kaiserslautern in 1993, directs much of the play from the middle, creating attacking options for his strikers.

Switzerland finished at the bottom of their group behind West Germany, Argentina, and Spain in the 1966 World Cup, and although a repeat is unlikely, their lack of experience at the highest level could prove to be their weakness. A good run in the World Cup would be a bonus for the Swiss FA, which is celebrating their centenary next year.

Route to the Finals

Europe: Group One

Switzerland	6	Estonia	0
Switzerland	3	Scotland	1
Switzerland	2	Italy	2
Switzerland	3	Malta	0
Switzerland	1	Portugal	1
Switzerland	2	Malta	0
Switzerland	1	Italy	0
Switzerland	1	Scotland	1
Portugal	1	Switzerland	0
Switzerland	4	Estonia	0

Played	Won	Drawn	Lost	Goals For	Goals Against	Pts.
10	6	3	1	23	6	15

Switzerland finished runners-up to Italy in Group One.

World Cup History

Switzerland reached the quarterfinals of the 1934 and 1938 World Cups. They put up a brave performance against eventual runner-up Czechoslovakia in 1934, only conceding the winning goal seven minutes from time, and were unfortunate to meet the eventual runner-up again, in the form of Hungary, four years later in Italy.

Switzerland took part in four of the first five tournaments after the war but were eliminated after the first round in all but one. Their most impressive performances came when they hosted the 1954 World Cup. Switzerland was the obvious choice as host, as FIFA was based in Zurich and 1954 represented FIFA's 50th anniversary. In the competition, they beat Italy twice to reach the quarterfinals but were then beaten in an extraordinary match against Austria. Leading 3–0 after 23 minutes, they eventually lost 7–5.

In 1966, two star players were suspended for staying out beyond curfew, and the team was subsequently thrashed 5–0 by West Germany in a game that saw the World Cup debut of Franz Beckenbauer.

Finals appearances: 6 (1934, 1938, 1950, 1954, 1962, 1966).
Biggest win: 4–1 vs. Italy (1954).
Biggest defeat: 5–7 vs. Austria (1954).
Leading scorer: Josef Hugi (6 goals).

RECORD

Played	Won	Draws	Lost	Goals For	Goals Against
18	5	2	11	28	44

• •

1934   **Eliminated second round**
First round: 3–2 vs. Holland; Second round: 2–3 vs. Czechoslovakia.

1938   **Eliminated second round**
First round: 1–1 vs. Germany, 4–2 vs. Germany (replay); Second round: 0–2 vs. Hungary.

1950   **Eliminated first round**
Group One: 0–3 vs. Yugoslavia, 2–2 vs. Brazil, 2–1 vs. Mexico.

1954   **Quarterfinalists**
Group Four: 2–1 vs. Italy, 0–2 vs. England, 4–1 vs.Italy (play-off); Quarterfinals: 5–7 vs. Austria.

1962   **Eliminated first round**
Group Two: 1–3 vs. Chile, 1–2 vs. West Germany, 0–3 vs. Italy.

1966   **Eliminated first round**
Group Two: 0–5 vs. West Germany, 1–2 vs. Spain, 0–2 vs. Argentina.

• •

GROUP B

BRAZIL, CAMEROON, RUSSIA, SWEDEN

Brazil heads a group containing Cameroon—the sensations of the 1990 World Cup—Russia, and Sweden. Brazil should feel confident of beating the Swedes and Russians, but the African side might show the traditional entertainers from South America a trick or two, and the game on June 24 should not be missed. This is a very tight group, although Brazil should head the final table, particularly with the great support of banging drums and samba dancing they are likely to attract. Competition for the second automatic qualification place will be intense.

GROUP B FIXTURES

Cameroon vs. Sweden	June 19 (Los Angeles)
Brazil vs. Russia	June 20 (San Francisco)
Brazil vs. Cameroon	June 24 (San Francisco)
Russia vs. Sweden	June 24 (Detroit)
Brazil vs. Sweden	June 28 (Detroit)
Russia vs. Cameroon	June 28 (San Francisco)

BRAZIL

Governing body: *Confederacao Brasilieri de Futebol.*
Formed: 1914.
Affiliated to FIFA: 1923.
National colors: Yellow shirts, blue shorts, white socks.
Manager/Coach: Carlos Alberta Parreira.

Winning the World Cup is an obsession for everyone involved in Brazilian football. They have entered and qualified for every tournament held, the only country to do so. For many people, a World Cup would simply not be the World Cup without the brilliant Brazilians. It is unthinkable that they should not be represented at the finals.

However, for the first time Brazil was, temporarily, under real pressure just to qualify for the final stages. A tied opening game with Ecuador and defeat against Bolivia—Brazil's first-ever defeat in a World Cup qualifier—meant that performances and results had to improve. They did, but it wasn't until the last three games, all at home, that they started to play with the style associated with Brazil. A revenge 6–0 victory over Bolivia, followed by victory over Venezuela led to a 2–0 win over Uruguay in front of a home crowd of 101,500.

Qualification lifted a tremendous weight off Carlos Alberto Parreria, the Brazilian manager, as he had lived the previous three months under the pressure of being the first manager to suffer a World Cup qualifying-game defeat. If Brazil also had failed to qualify, one cannot imagine what his fate would have been at the hands of a soccer-mad public.

The key to the final game was the return of Romario to the national team after nearly nine months' absence following disciplinary measures. The temperamental striker, who plays club football for Barcelona in Spain, was recalled as a result of public demand. He scored both goals in a stunning display that prompted the Brazilian manager to claim that Romario was a genius and one of the best forwards in the world.

He will very much be a player to watch in the finals, as he is deadly in front of the goal and blessed with exceptional skill. His pace, timing, and ability to score the most spectacular goals make him a favorite with football fans and, at 27, he is now approaching his peak.

Although he is a brilliant striker, he has created problems for his coaches and managers—avoiding training, flying back to Rio at short notice—but there is absolutely no doubt that if Romario is in the mood he can win games single-handed.

Brazil will be many people's favorite to win the tournament again this year. The attacking flair and skills of Romario, Rai, and Bebeto are sufficient to score plenty of goals, and if Dunga, Branco, and Ricardo Rocha can also add defensive solidity to the team, they could challenge for the title.

Route to the Finals

South America: Group B

Ecuador	0	Brazil	0
Bolivia	2	Brazil	0
Brazil	5	Venezuela	1
Brazil	1	Uruguay	1
Brazil	2	Ecuador	0
Brazil	6	Bolivia	0
Brazil	4	Venezuela	0
Brazil	2	Uruguay	0

Played	Won	Drawn	Lost	Goals For	Goals Against	Pts.
8	5	2	1	20	4	12

Brazil won Group B.

World Cup History

Believed to have been introduced by British railway workers in Sao Paulo at the end of the 19th century, soccer quickly caught on, with the proliferation of leagues throughout the country. However, selecting a national team from all of the different leagues proved difficult, particularly with the huge distances involved in traveling to games, and this was the main reason Brazil was slow in taking up international soccer. This makes their success in the World Cup all the more remarkable.

Brazil was knocked out in the first round of both the 1930 and 1934 tournaments, but reached the semifinals four years later. There, they committed the error of resting their star striker, Leonidas, against Italy, believing that they would reach the final. This self-assurance proved costly, as Italy scored twice to win the match.

In 1950, Brazil, the host, was the overwhelming favorite to win but, requiring only a draw, they continued to play attacking football when they could have defended a lead, and allowed Uruguay to score twice and snatch the title.

The 1954 quarterfinal defeat against Hungary is perhaps best forgotten. It was sad that a game between the two best attacking teams should prove to be one of the most violent games in the history of the competition.

In 1958 the World Cup was Brazil's at long last, inspired by Didi, Garrincha, and a 17-year-old prodigy called Pele. In Chile, 1962, it belonged to them again, but not to Pele, who was injured in the second game and missed the rest of the tournament. Amarildo proved a marvelous replacement, but the show belonged to Garrincha.

Pele again did not have a happy time in 1966, when Brazil lost their crown to England. He threatened never to play in the World Cup again, but thankfully he was to join the likes of Tostao, Gerson, Rivelino, and Jairzinho for the 1970 finals.

The team that won the World Cup in Mexico was one of the best ever to take the field in a World Cup. Apart from England, no one came close to matching the sublime skills of the Brazilians.

Since 1970, the national team has reverted to a more defensive style, and it was only in 1982 that Brazil produced a team that promised the same supreme footballing skills of old. Falcao, Socrates, and Zico played with the style reminiscent of the golden era, but lost to Italy, the eventual champion, in a classic encounter. Requiring only a draw, Brazil again paid the penalty of pressing forward to win the game.

Finals appearances: All 14.
Biggest win: 7–1 vs. Sweden (1950).
Biggest defeat: 2–4 vs. Hungary (1954).
Leading scorer: Pele (12 goals).

RECORD

Played	Won	Draws	Lost	Goals For	Goals Against
66	44	10	12	148	65

● ●

1930 **Eliminated first round**
Group Two: 1–2 vs.Yugoslavia, 4–0 vs.Bolivia.
1934 **Eliminated first round**
First round: 1–3 vs.Spain.
1938 **THIRD PLACE**
First round: 6–5 vs.Poland; Second round: 1–1 vs. Czechoslovakia, 2–1 vs. Czechoslovakia (replay);

Semifinal: 1–2 vs.Italy; Third-place play-off:
4–2 vs.Sweden.

1950   RUNNERS-UP
Group One: 4–0 vs.Mexico, 2–2 vs. Switzerland,
2–0 vs. Yugoslavia; Final pool: 7–1 vs. Sweden,
6–1 vs. Spain, 1–2 vs. Uruguay.

1954   Quarterfinalists
Group One: 5–0 vs. Mexico, 1–1 vs. Yugoslavia;
Quarterfinals: 2–4 vs. Hungary.

1958   WINNERS
Group Four: 3–0 vs. Austria, 0–0 vs. England,
2–0 vs. Soviet Union; Quarterfinal: 1–0 vs. Wales;
Semifinal: 5–2 vs. France; Final: 5–2 vs. Sweden.

1962   WINNERS
Group Three: 2–0 vs. Mexico, 0–0 vs. Czechoslovakia,
2–1 vs. Spain; Quarterfinal: 3–1 vs. England;
Semifinal: 4–2 vs. Chile; Final: 3–1 vs. Czechoslovakia

1966   Eliminated first round
Group Three: 2–0 vs. Bulgaria, 1–3 vs. Hungary,
1–3 vs. Portugal.

1970   WINNERS
Group Three: 4–1 vs. Czechoslovakia, 1–0 vs.
England, 3–2 vs. Romania; Quarterfinal: 4–2 vs.
Peru; Semifinal: 3–1 vs. Uruguay; Final: 4–1 vs. Italy.

1974   FOURTH PLACE
Group Two: 0–0 vs. Yugoslavia, 0–0 vs.
Scotland, 3–0 vs. Zaire; Group A: 1–0 vs. East
Germany, 2–1 vs. Argentina, 0–2 vs. Holland;
Third-place play-off: 0–1 vs. Poland.

1978   THIRD PLACE
Group Three: 1–1 vs. Sweden, 0–0 vs. Spain,
1–0 vs. Austria; Group B: 3–0 vs. Peru, 0–0 vs.
Argentina, 3–1 vs. Poland; Third-place play-off:
2–1 vs. Italy.

1982   **Eliminated second round**
Group Six: 2–1 vs. Soviet Union, 4–1 vs.
Scotland, 4–0 vs. New Zealand; Group C: 3–1
vs. Argentina, 2–3 vs. Italy.

1986   **Quarterfinalists**
Group D: 1–0 vs. Spain, 1–0 vs. Algeria, 3–0 vs.
Northern Ireland; Second round: 4–0 vs. Poland,
1–1 vs. France (3–4 in penalties).

1990   **Eliminated second round**
Group C: 2–1 vs. Sweden, 1–0 vs. Costa Rica,
1–0 vs. Scotland; Second round: 0–1 vs. Argentina.

● ●

CAMEROON

Governing body: *Federation Camerounaise de Football*.
Formed: 1960.
Affiliated to FIFA: 1962.
National colors: Green shirts, red shorts, yellow socks.
Manager/Coach: Henri Michel.

Cameroon is probably the most celebrated of all of Africa's
teams. There was widespread rejoicing when they beat
Argentina 1–0 in the opening game of the 1990 World
Cup, a victory that will go down as one of the biggest
upsets ever, along with the United States' win over
England in 1950, North Korea's win over Italy in 1966,
and West Germany's defeat against Algeria in 1982.

Cameroon's performance in those finals was probably
the highlight of the tournament, although the quality
and vigor of their tackling often left a lot to be desired.

Except for conceding two careless penalties against England, they were only 10 minutes away from reaching the semifinals.

More importantly, though, they had shown that African football was a force to be reckoned with—a major consideration when FIFA awarded a third qualification place to Africa for the 1994 finals.

Cameroon qualified for the United States World Cup with something to spare. Oman Biyik, scorer of that memorable goal against Argentina, is still around and scored two early goals in the decisive qualifier against Zimbabwe, but was later injured. He will be around to lead the Cameroon attack. The victory that sealed qualification set off wild celebrations around the country, and a public holiday was declared.

A new coach, Jean Pierre Zadi, was appointed in October 1993, but was replaced by Henri Michel in January of this year. Michel, the one–time head of the French national team, will need to regain the team confidence that followed their extraordinary success in 1990 if they are to repeat the feat. Constant bickering over salaries and bonuses has created a lack of unity within the team that will make his job that much harder.

Even at the age of 42, Roger Milla is said to be contemplating a comeback for the World Cup finals. It would be an extraordinary achievement, one that would thrill millions of people who watched his performances in 1990, and particularly his unique way of celebrating scoring goals.

Route to the Finals

Africa: First-round Group B

Cameroon	5	Swaziland	0
Cameroon	2	Zaire	1

Swaziland	0	Cameroon	0
Cameroon	0	Zaire	0

Played	Won	Drawn	Lost	Goals For	Goals Against	Pts.
4	2	2	0	7	1	6

Second-round Group C

Cameroon	3	Guinea	1
Zimbabwe	1	Cameroon	0
Cameroon	1	Guinea	0
Cameroon	3	Zimbabwe	1.

Played	Won	Drawn	Lost	Goals For	Goals Against	Pts.
4	3	0	1	7	3	6

Cameroon won Group C.

World Cup History

In 1982, with Roger Milla as their star player, Cameroon went out of the tournament despite remaining unbeaten. Italy, the eventual World Cup winner, only qualified for the second round by virtue of having scored one more goal than Cameroon.

Then followed their memorable victory over Argentina in 1990, achieved despite their being reduced to only nine men at the end of the game. Massing was sent off with only two minutes to go for a cynical tackle, but the referee had already sent off Kana Biyik when it appeared that he had not even committed a foul. But, as often happens, injustice spurred the team on, and it was Kana's brother, Oman Biyik, who scored the winning goal only five minutes later.

Cameroon confirmed their passage to the second round with a 2–1 win against Romania. The hero was Roger Milla, who had come out of semiretirement for the tournament and, at 38, became the oldest man to score in the World Cup. It was Milla again who, after coming on as a substitute, inspired the Africans to a 2–1 victory over Colombia. But in the quarterfinals, despite leading England 2–1, they committed two unnecessary offenses in the penalty area and England's Lineker scored both times from the penalty spot.

Cameroon was out, but they had delighted everyone with their style and approach to the game.

Finals appearances: 2 (1982, 1990).
Biggest win: 2–1 vs. Romania (1990), 2–1 vs. Colombia (1990).
Biggest defeat: 0–4 vs. Soviet Union (1990).
Leading scorer: Roger Milla (4 goals).

RECORD					
Played	Won	Drawn	Lost	Goals For	Goals Against
8	3	3	2	8	10

• •

1982   **Eliminated first round**
Group One: 0–0 vs. Peru, 0–0 vs. Poland, 1–1 vs. Italy.
1990   **Quarterfinalists**
Group B: 1–0 vs. Argentina, 2–1 vs. Romania, 0–4 vs. Soviet Union; Second round: 2–1 vs. Colombia; Quarterfinals: 2–3 vs. England.

• •

RUSSIA

Governing body: Russian Football Union.
Formed: 1991.
National colors: White shirts, blue shorts, red socks.
Manager/Coach: Pavel Sadyrin.

It is all change for the former USSR. The Commonwealth of Independent States has been disbanded, and Russia is the only team to have qualified for the finals. Countries such as Belarus and Ukraine were too late to apply to qualify for the 1994 World Cup finals and must wait for the 1998 finals.

Qualification for the finals was made easier for Russia by the withdrawal of Yugoslavia from Group Five. Their only defeat was at the hands of group-winner Greece, but both teams were safely through by then, so the result was academic.

Player unrest raised its head early this year when a group of players threatened to withdraw from the national squad unless Pavel Sadyrin was replaced by Anatoli Bishovets, the former national coach. They claimed that Sadyrin was a good club coach but did not fit the standards of a national coach. They said that Russia's qualification for the World Cup was a result of the work done by Bishovets, who had been forced to resign after the poor showing of Russia (then the CIS) in the European Championship.

The players also complained of the poor training facilities, but the Russian Federation denied the charges and continued to support Sadyrin. Deputy Federation head Nikita Simonyan said that Sadyrin would lead the squad into the finals and remain in his post until his contract runs out.

Russia has always produced a technically proficient team, but if they have had a flaw in the past it is that they come apart under pressure, which might explain why they fail to live up to expectation at major tournaments. At the World Cup finals in 1990, for example, they were considered to be one of the strongest second-seeded teams, but team discipline fell apart after a loss to Argentina.

They do possess some exciting players, however. Sergei Kiriakov is one of the emerging talents and is definitely a player to look out for. He moved to his current club, Karlsruhe in the German Bundesliga, from Moscow Dynamo for a modest $950,000 but is now valued at 10 times that figure. The 24-year-old's main assets are his speed, close control, accurate crosses, and shooting power, and he has become something of a cult figure in Germany, as he is always willing to try and score spectacular goals such as bicycle kicks.

Shalimov and Yuran will give the team a touch of class, and Kanchelskis, who plays for the English Premier league champions, Manchester United, will be using his tremendous pace and close control to run at and unsettle defenses. Russia's goalkeeper, Kharin, also plays in the English Premier league, for Chelsea.

This creates a problem that is common to many national coaches. So many members of their squad playing for foreign clubs severely limits the amount of time a coach can work with his selections to hone them into a coordinated unit.

On the whole this is a difficult team to assess, as their qualifying group was very weak and they have yet to face top-class opposition in a competitive game. However one hopes that their players will sort out their differences and not boycott the finals.

Route to the Finals

Europe: Group Five

Russia	1	Iceland	0
Russia	2	Luxembourg	0
Russia	4	Luxembourg	0
Russia	3	Hungary	0
Russia	1	Greece	1
Russia	1	Iceland	1
Russia	3	Hungary	1
Greece	1	Russia	0

Played	Won	Drawn	Lost	Goals For	Goals Against	Pts.
8	5	2	1	15	4	12

Russia finished runners-up to Greece in Group Five.

World Cup History

(As the former Soviet Union)

Football was introduced to Soviet cotton workers as early as the 1880s by the English Charnock brothers. The major clubs were centered around Moscow, and a league was formed in the 1930s, but the Soviet Union did not enter international football until the 1950s. They won the 1956 Olympic tournament and in their World Cup debut faced a tough opening group containing England, Brazil, and Austria. A 1–0 victory over England in a play-off took them to a quarterfinal clash against host Sweden. They lost, but had shown they were a fit and organized team with some notable players such as Lev Yashin and Valentin Ivanov.

The Soviet Union again lost in the quarterfinals to the host, this time Chile, in 1962, but gained revenge in

1966, beating Chile in the opening round on their way to a semifinal meeting with West Germany. They had a powerful side, with Yashin superb in goal, but they had to be content with fourth as Haller and Beckenbauer settled the game for the West Germans.

Elimination at the quarterfinal stage in 1970 was followed by failure to qualify for the next two finals and since then the Soviet team has promised much in early rounds, only to fail at the next hurdle.

Finals appearances: 7 (1958, 1962, 1966, 1970, 1982, 1986, 1990).
Biggest win: 6–0 vs. Hungary (1986).
Biggest defeat: 3–4 vs. Belgium (1986).
Leading scorer: Valentin Ivanov (5 goals).

RECORD

Played	Won	Drawn	Lost	Goals For	Goals Against
31	15	6	10	53	34

● ●

1958   Quarterfinalists
Group Four: 2–2 vs. England, 2–0 vs. Austria, 0–2 vs. Brazil; Play-off: 1–0 vs. England; Quarterfinal: 0–2 vs. Sweden.

1962   Quarterfinalists
Group One: 2–0 vs. Yugoslavia, 4–4 vs. Colombia, 2–1 vs. Uruguay; Quarterfinal: 1–2 vs. Chile.

1966   FOURTH PLACE
Group Four: 3–0 vs. North Korea, 1–0 vs. Italy,

2–1 vs. Chile; Quarterfinal: 2–1 vs. Hungary;
Semifinal: 1–2 vs. West Germany; Third-place
play-off: 1–2 vs. Portugal.

1970 **Quarterfinalists**
Group One: 0–0 vs. Mexico, 4–1 vs. Belgium,
2–0 vs. El Salvador; Quarterfinal: 0–1 vs. Uruguay.

1982 **Eliminated second round**
Group Six: 1–2 vs. Brazil, 3–0 vs. New Zealand,
2–2 vs. Scotland; Group A: 1–0 vs. Belgium,
0–0 vs. Poland.

1986 **Eliminated second round**
Group C: 6–0 vs. Hungary, 1–1 vs. France, 2–0
vs. Canada; Second round: 3–4 vs. Belgium.

1990 **Eliminated first round**
Group B: 0–2 vs. Romania, 0–2 vs. Argentina,
4–0 vs. Cameroon.

● ●

SWEDEN

Governing body: *Svenska Fotbollfoerbundet*.
Founded: 1904.
Affiliated to FIFA: 1904.
National colors: Yellow shirts, blue shorts, yellow socks.
Manager/Coach: Tommy Svensson.

Sweden's qualification was somewhat overshadowed by
France's amazing collapse in the same qualifying group.
Sweden began with three successive victories and despite
an unlucky 2–1 loss to France, they remained on course
to qualify from Group Six. They drew three of their last

four qualifying games; but victory in the other, at home in front of a capacity crowd against Finland, was sufficient to confirm their place in the finals.

The Swedes are a very organized team defensively, very disciplined, and retain much of the squad that performed so well to reach the semifinals of the European Championships in 1992. Jonas Thern brings drive to the midfield and Stefan Rehn is a creative playmaker, but it is in attack that Sweden may well be at their most dangerous. The trio of Martin Dahlin, Tomas Brolin, and Kennet Andersson provides a lethal mix of predatory instinct, skill, and shooting power.

Martin Dahlin's contribution to Sweden's qualification cannot be underestimated. His seven goals, scored at crucial times, were a key factor. He scored equalizing goals against Bulgaria and France, the last with only three minutes remaining in the game. Dahlin, voted Swedish Player of the Year, plays for Borussia Monchengladbach and is regarded as one of Europe's top strikers. His tremendous pace and strength make it very difficult for defenders to get the ball off him.

Brolin's decision to pull out of Sweden's national team a few days before the vital World Cup qualifier against Finland astounded Swedish football. It appeared to be a reaction to some unfavorable publicity in the Swedish press, but his absence would be a major blow to the Swedish team were he not to play in the United States. He has proved himself as a top out-and-out striker, but since joining Parma in Italy he has developed into a tough, attacking all-arounder with the ability to play in various positions.

•   •   •

Route to the Finals

Europe: Group Six

Sweden	1	Finland	0
Sweden	2	Bulgaria	0
Sweden	3	Israel	1
France	2	Sweden	1
Sweden	1	Austria	0
Sweden	5	Israel	0
Sweden	1	France	1
Sweden	1	Bulgaria	1
Sweden	3	Finland	2
Sweden	1	Austria	1

Played	Won	Drawn	Lost	Goals For	Goals Against	Pts.
10	6	3	1	19	8	15

Sweden won Group Six.

World Cup History

Sweden joined FIFA as one of the founding members in 1904, and the national team competed in the 1908 Olympic Games. The country took part in the 1934 and 1938 World Cup finals, but gained their biggest successes after the war.

The 1940s had seen Sweden grow as a football power, and after winning the 1948 Olympic tournament and incurring Italy's first World Cup defeat in the 1950 World Cup finals, many of their best players were bought by big Italian clubs. George Raynor, the English manager of the national team, was largely responsible for Sweden's success during this period, and guided them to their most outstanding achievement—the final of the 1958 World Cup. They lost to Brazil, but this was no disgrace, as the South Americans were on the brink of an outstanding period.

Since then Sweden has had a rather modest time in World Cup finals. They qualified for three finals in the 1970s but only progressed to the second round in 1974. In the last tournament, they did not do themselves justice, losing all of their first-round games.

Finals appearances: 8 (1934, 1938, 1950, 1958, 1970, 1974, 1978, 1990).
Biggest win: 8–0 vs. Cuba (1938).
Biggest defeat: 1–7 vs. Brazil (1950).
Leading scorers: Gustav Wetterstrom, Kurt Hamrin, Agne Simonsson, Sven Jonasson, Ralf Edstrom (4 goals).

RECORD

Played	Won	Drawn	Lost	Goals For	Goals Against
31	11	6	14	51	52

● ●

1934 **Quarterfinalists**
First round: 3–2 vs. Argentina; Second round: 1–2 vs. Germany.
1938 **FOURTH PLACE**
First round: bye; Second round: 8–0 vs. Cuba; Semifinal: 1–5 vs. Hungary; Third-place play-off: 2–4 vs. Brazil.

1950 **THIRD PLACE**
Group Three: 3–2 vs. Italy, 2–2 vs. Paraguay;
Final pool: 1–7 vs. Brazil, 2–3 vs. Uruguay, 3–1
vs. Spain.

1958 **RUNNERS-UP**
Group Three: 3–0 vs. Mexico, 2–1 vs. Hungary,
0–0 vs. Wales; Quarterfinal: 2–0 vs. Soviet
Union; Semifinal: 3–1 vs. West Germany; Final:
2–5 vs. Brazil.

1970 **Eliminated first round**
Group Two: 0–1 vs. Italy, 1–1 vs. Israel, 1–0 vs.
Uruguay.

1974 **Eliminated second round**
Group Three: 0–0 vs. Bulgaria, 0–0 vs. Holland,
3–0 vs. Uruguay; Group B: 0–1 vs. Poland, 2–4
vs. West Germany, 2–1 vs. Yugoslavia.

1978 **Eliminated first round**
Group Three: 1–1 vs. Brazil, 0–1 vs. Austria,
0–1 vs. Spain.

1990 **Eliminated first round**
Group C: 1–2 vs. Brazil, 1–2 vs. Scotland, 1–2
vs. Costa Rica.

● ●

GROUP C

GERMANY, BOLIVIA, SPAIN, SOUTH KOREA

The opening game of the tournament is always tricky. Germany, the Cup holders, will want to impress the millions of viewers, but will also have to guard against underestimating their opponents. Bolivia will undoubtedly raise their game, but it is hard to see Germany not winning by a comfortable margin. Spain beat South Korea 3–1 four years ago, and the experienced European side should take second place in front of South Korea, who have yet to win a game in the finals.

GROUP C FIXTURES

Germany vs. Bolivia	June 17 (Chicago)
Spain vs. South Korea	June 17 (Dallas)
Germany vs. Spain	June 21 (Chicago)
Bolivia vs. South Korea	June 23 (Boston)
Germany vs. South Korea	June 27 (Dallas)
Bolivia vs. Spain	June 27 (Chicago)

GERMANY

Governing body: *Deutsche Fussball–Bund.*
Founded: 1900.
Affiliated to FIFA: 1904–1946; 1950.
National colors: White shirts (black, red, and orange shoulders), black shorts, white socks.
Manager/Coach: Berti Vogts.

As holder of the World Cup, Germany automatically qualifies for the 1994 tournament. This has given manager Berti Vogts plenty of time in which to experiment with new players and tactics, but it is also true that Germany has missed out on the sort of competitive matches that qualification for a tournament provides. No matter how many friendlies you play, there is no substitute for competitive football.

However, there is little doubt that Vogts will have his team fit and prepared to continue Germany's magnificent tradition in the World Cup. Vogts, who has been in charge since 1990, believes that Germany is playing the type of football he wants. The lapses that cost them goals in the U.S. Cup '93 were not serious, and he will have a strong defensive lineup with key players rested and prepared.

Germany did not go to the U.S. Cup '93 just for the ride. They treated it as a serious dress rehearsal for the real thing. They wanted to win it, and win it they did. Coming back from 0–3 down to Brazil to draw 3–3 was typical of the German resilience.

Three-time winners and three-time runners-up, the holders are competing as unified Germany for the first time since 1938. They still have their inspirational captain Lothar Matthaus, who has now won every honor in football, including becoming only the second German player, after Franz Beckenbauer, to reach 100 international caps. His surging runs and powerful shooting in midfield were a feature of the 1990 World Cup–winning team, but he is now playing as a sweeper in defense. His great vision and reading of the game will be crucial to Germany, but his move has also had the double advantage of allowing Andy Moller to shine in midfield. He could be the German's star of the tournament.

Moller did not play a large part in Germany's 1990 success, but now, at the age of 26, he has developed into a skillful, attacking midfielder and has been in consistently good form for his Italian club Juventus. Initially an inconsistent performer, he has matured in the past few seasons and now deploys his outstanding creative skills to their full potential. With Guido Buchwald holding a more "defensive" role in midfield, Moller has the space to create scoring opportunities for the strikers, Karl-Heinz Riedle and Jurgen Klinsmann.

In one of their buildup games, Germany beat a somewhat depleted Brazilian side, 2–1, in Cologne, with Moller giving an inspirational performance and scoring the winning goal. This was only the third time Germany has beaten Brazil in 15 meetings between these two great footballing nations in the past 30 years. Moller was probably the best player in the game.

Germany has a wealth of midfield talent with Hassler, Sammer, Doll, and Effenberg all competing alongside Moller.

And yet another player who may make his mark in this position in the United States tournament is Christian Ziege. If not this year, then he is definitely a name for the future. One of the youngest members of the national squad, Ziege is at his most effective on the left side of midfield. He is thought to be a potential mainstay of the German team for the next 10 years and has the makings of a truly great footballer with pace, control, and excellent technique. He played in the U.S. Cup '93 and nearly scored against England, hitting the post after an excellent run from deep, which allowed Jurgen Klinsmann to score from the rebound.

However, a shocking loss to Argentina in Miami last December made a number of people question the standard of the German team. They fielded what was to all intents and purposes a full-strength team and lost to an Argentinian side that did not have most of their established players.

But it is never wise to underestimate the Germans. They have reached the last three finals, an amazingly consistent achievement. The great Franz Beckenbauer put the German's success down to a strong mentality, and they are certainly a team against whom it is best to remember the phrase "It's not over till the fat lady sings."

They have a knack of pacing themselves through the tournament, improving as it progresses, and they will be there when the money's down.

Route to the Finals
Qualified automatically as champions.

World Cup History
Three World Cup victories and appearances in six World Cup finals, including the last three, is a record that no other country can match. For sheer consistency, Germany has been the outstanding team since the Second World War.

Despite finishing third in the 1934 tournament, beating the Austrian "Wunderteam," Germany began their World Cup campaign quietly. Germany was excluded from the 1950 tournament by FIFA as a result of the war, but four years later they were world champions and had completed one of the most amazing turnarounds in soccer history.

The Hungarian team of 1954 was considered the best in the world, and yet the Germans beat them in a scintillating final that saw Hungary take a quick 2-0 lead, only for the Germans to reply with a goal from Morlock and two from Rahn. This established a great German tradition of resilience and a never-say-die attitude.

Semifinalists in 1958 and quarterfinalists in 1962, West Germany next appeared in the final in 1966. In the most controversial final in World Cup history, the host, England, held a 2–1 lead with seconds to go. But West Germany persevered and snatched an equalizer in the dying seconds to send the game into extra time. England won with two goals by Geoff Hurst.

In 1963 a new national league, the Bundesliga, had been created, which undoubtedly improved the quality of the club teams. Bayern Munich was the dominant team and formed the basis of the national team, which became the dominant force in world football.

In 1974 a team consisting of Gerd Muller, Franz Beckenbauer, and Sepp Maier won the World Cup. Since then the Germans have continued their great World Cup tradition by reaching the finals in 1982, 1986, and 1990. Each World Cup witnesses new players stepping in to carry on where the last ones left off—great teams with inspirational leaders.

Finals appearances: 12 (1934, 1938 as Germany, 1954, 1958, 1962, 1966, 1970, 1974, 1978, 1982, 1986, 1990 as West Germany).
Biggest win: 7–2 vs. Turkey (1954).
Biggest defeat: 3–8 vs. Hungary (1954).
Leading scorer: Gerd Muller (14 goals).

RECORD

Played	Won	Drawn	Lost	Goals For	Goals Against
68	42	12	14	145	90

• •

1934   **THIRD PLACE**
First round: 5–2 vs. Belgium; Second round: 2–1
vs. Sweden; Semifinal: 1–3 vs. Czechoslovakia;
Third-place play-off: 3–2 vs. Austria.

1938   **Eliminated first round**
First round:1–1 vs. Switzerland, 2–4 vs.
Switzerland (replay).

1954   **WINNERS**
Group Two: 4–1 vs. Turkey, 3–8 vs. Hungary, 7–2
vs. Turkey (play-off); Quarterfinal: 2–0 vs.
Yugoslavia; Semifinal: 6–1 vs. Austria; Final: 3–2
vs. Hungary.

1958   **FOURTH PLACE**
Group One: 3–1 vs. Argentina, 2–2 vs.
Czechoslovakia, 2–2 vs. Northern Ireland;
Quarterfinal: 1–0 vs. Yugoslavia; Semifinal: 1–3
vs. Sweden; Third-place play-off: 3–6 vs. France.

1962   **Quarterfinalists**
Group Two: 0–0 vs. Italy, 2–1 vs. Switzerland,
2–0 vs. Chile; Quarterfinals: 0–1 vs. Yugoslavia.

1966   **RUNNERS-UP**
Group Two: 5–0 vs. Switzerland, 0–0 vs.
Argentina, 2–1 vs. Spain; Quarterfinal: 4–0 vs.
Uruguay; Semifinal: 2–1 vs. Soviet Union; Final:
2–4 vs. England.

1970   **THIRD PLACE**
Group Four: 2–1 vs. Morocco, 5–2 vs. Bulgaria;
3–1 vs. Peru; Quarterfinal: 3–2 vs. England;
Semifinal: 3–4 vs. Italy; Third-place play-off: 1–0
vs. Uruguay.

1974   **WINNERS**
Group One: 1–0 vs. Chile, 3–0 vs. Australia, 0–1

vs. East Germany; Group B: 2–0 vs. Yugoslavia, 4–2 vs. Sweden, 1–0 vs. Poland; Final: 2–1 vs. Holland.

1978   Eliminated second round

Group Two: 0–0 vs. Poland, 6–0 vs. Mexico, 0–0 vs. Tunisia; Group A: 0–0 vs. Italy, 2–2 vs. Holland, 2–3 vs. Austria.

1982   RUNNERS-UP

Group Two: 1–2 vs. Algeria, 4–1 vs. Chile, 1–0 vs. Austria; Group B: 0–0 vs. England, 2–1 vs. Spain; Semifinal: 3–3 vs. France (5–4 on penalties); Final: 1–3 vs. Italy.

1986   RUNNERS-UP

Group E: 1–1 vs. Uruguay, 2–1 vs. Scotland, 0–2 vs. Denmark; Second round: 1–0 vs. Morocco; Quarterfinal: 0–0 vs. Mexico (4–1 on penalties); Semifinal: 2–0 vs. France; Final: 2–3 vs. Argentina.

1990   WINNERS

Group D: 4–1 vs. Yugoslavia, 5–1 vs. United Arab Emirates, 1–1 vs. Colombia; Second round: 2–1 vs. Holland; Quarterfinal: 1–0 vs. Czechoslovakia; Semifinal: 1–1 vs. England (4–3 on penalties); Final: 1–0 vs. Argentina.

● ●

BOLIVIA

Governing body: *Federation Boliviana de Futbol.*
Founded: 1925.
Affiliated to FIFA: 1926.
National colors: Green shirts, white shorts, white socks.
Manager/Coach: Javier Azkargorta.

If the magnitude of the event does not affect their confidence, Bolivia, a youthful team of developing talent, could spring one or two surprises. As Argentina discovered in 1990 when they lost to unfavored Cameroon, the emerging nations can rise to the occasion and cause an upset.

However, no matter how much Bolivian football has developed, there is no doubt that their qualification came as a result of playing their home games at altitude. The advantage to the Bolivian players, who are used to the thin air, is enormous, and it is significant that after winning all their home games, Bolivia failed to win any of their final three games—all away from home.

What cannot be taken away from them is the distinction of becoming the first team ever to inflict a qualifying-round defeat on Brazil—an achievement celebrated in La Paz as if they had won the World Cup itself.

In that memorable victory, Brazil appeared to have overcome the problems of altitude, but with two minutes to go, Marco Etcheverry got to the goal line and, even though there were no Bolivians in the six-yard area to meet his cross, Taffarel, the Brazilian goalkeeper, deflected the ball into his own net. Pena raced through to score a second goal in the dying seconds.

Much will be expected by Bolivian fans of the team's playmaker, Erwin Sanchez. He is the only member of the squad to play for a European club, Boavista in Portugal, and he scored four goals in the qualifying rounds and created many more.

Spanish coach Javier Azkargorta has managed to improve the squad, and they performed well in the South American Championship, where they drew with Mexico, the finalists, and Colombia, and only lost 1–0 to Argentina, the eventual winners.

FIFA has since banned games at such altitude, which may have serious implications for Bolivia to qualify for future tournaments. The players have little or no experience at the highest level and even a nothing-to-lose mentality will not be enough to see them qualify for the second round.

Route to the Finals

South America: Group B

Bolivia	7	Venezuela	1
Bolivia	2	Brazil	0
Bolivia	3	Uruguay	0
Bolivia	1	Ecuador	0
Bolivia	7	Venezuela	0
Brazil	6	Bolivia	0
Uruguay	2	Bolivia	1
Bolivia	1	Ecuador	1

Played	Won	Drawn	Lost	Goals For	Goals Against	Pts.
8	5	1	2	22	10	11

Bolivia finished runners-up to Brazil.

World Cup History

The first Bolivian soccer club was founded in 1896, but the game spread slowly throughout the country. Although they sent a team to the 1930 World Cup, losses to Yugoslavia and Brazil were not surprising. An inexperienced team qualified for the 1950 finals but was beaten convincingly by Uruguay.

Bolivia has performed creditably in the qualifying stages of the World Cup, mainly as a result of playing their home games at altitude. However, their form away from home has let them down, until now.

Finals appearances: 2 (1930, 1950).
Biggest win: Has never won.
Biggest defeat: 0–8 vs. Uruguay.
Leading scorer: Has never scored.

RECORD

Played	Won	Drawn	Lost	Goals For	Goals Against
3	0	0	3	0	16

• •

1930 **Eliminated first round**
Group Two: 0–4 vs. Yugoslavia, 0–4 vs. Brazil.
1950 **Eliminated first round**
Group Four: 0–8 vs. Uruguay.

• •

SPAIN

Governing body: *Real Federacion Espanola de Futbol.*
Founded: 1913.
Affiliated to FIFA: 1904.
National colors: Red shirts, blue shorts, blue socks.
Manager/Coach: Javier Clemente.

One of the most glamorous of soccer nations, Spain qualified from their group with a strong finish, beating the Republic of Ireland in Dublin and winning a brave, battling 1–0 victory over Denmark despite having their influential goalkeeper and captain, Andoni Zubizaretta, sent off after only 10 minutes—some way to celebrate becoming his country's most-capped player. Fernando Hierro scored with a header after 63 minutes to confirm Spain as qualifiers.

Spain will go to the States as something of an unknown quantity, both in terms of play and the composition of the squad. Coach Javier Clemente used 36 players in the qualifying games, preferring to adapt the team to suit the opposition. He must now narrow down his options to develop a squad that is flexible enough to take on the widely varying opposition they will meet.

They may not be the strongest contenders, but Clemente appears to have opted for youth instead of experience. He has made sweeping changes to the team since taking over, and this appears to signal the end of the international careers of Michel and Butragueno—despite Michel having one of his best-ever seasons for Real Madrid.

With players of the quality of Salinas, Luis Enrique, and Caminero, they should display a bit of style. And with Ferrer, a tenacious defender who supports the attack well, and Guerrero, the potential golden boy of Spanish soccer, Clemente may have achieved a balanced team.

There is a clublike atmosphere within the squad, and in Clemente, they have an astute and confident coach. Clemente was delighted with the draw, which pits Spain against South Korea in Dallas, and then Germany followed by Bolivia in Chicago. The opponents and venues are just what he wanted, and he believes that something serious would have to go wrong for Spain not to qualify for the second round.

Route to the Finals

Europe: Group 3

Spain	3	Albania	0
Spain	0	Latvia	0
Spain	0	Northern Ireland	0
Spain	0	Republic of Ireland	0
Spain	5	Latvia	0
Spain	5	Lithuania	0
Denmark	1	Spain	0
Spain	3	Northern Ireland	1
Spain	2	Lithuania	0
Spain	5	Albania	1
Spain	3	Republic of Ireland	1
Spain	1	Denmark	0

Played	Won	Drawn	Lost	Goals For	Goals Against	Pts.
12	8	3	1	27	4	19

Spain won Group 3.

World Cup History

Spanish clubs Real Madrid and Barcelona are two of the biggest and most famous clubs in the world, and regular contenders for major European honors. Together with Atletico Madrid, they have often supplied the majority of the national team but, as yet, they have seldom lived up to their promise.

Spain's best performance in a World Cup was fourth place in Brazil in 1950, when they beat the United States, Chile, and England. After a lean spell, the national team qualified for Chile in 1962 and England in 1966—a period that saw Real Madrid dominate European football—but they were not quite the match of teams such as Brazil and West Germany.

However, the biggest blow to the fanatical Spanish public was their poor display when, as hosts in 1982, they were considered one of the pre-tournament favorites. In one of the worst performances by a host country, Spain struggled through the first round, and despite a highly talented team of individuals, they had problems playing as a team and crashed out of the tournament.

In subsequent tournaments Spain has shown what they are capable of, particularly in a 5–1 victory over Denmark, who until then had been the revelation of the 1986 finals. After this, they were unlucky to lose to Belgium in a penalty shoot-out.

Finals appearances: 8 (1934, 1950, 1962, 1966, 1978, 1982, 1986, 1990).

Biggest win: 5–1 vs. Denmark (1986).

Biggest defeat: 1–6 vs. Brazil (1950).

Leading scorers: Estanislao Basora, Emilio Butragueno (5 goals).

RECORD

Played	Won	Drawn	Lost	Goals For	Goals Against
32	13	6	13	43	38

• •

1934 **Eliminated second round**
First round: 3–1 vs. Brazil; Second round: 1–1 vs. Italy, 0–1 vs. Italy (replay).

1950 **FOURTH PLACE**
Group Two: 3–1 vs. United States, 2–0 vs. Chile, 1–0 vs. England; Final pool: 2–2 vs. Uruguay, 1–6 vs. Brazil, 1–3 vs. Sweden.

1962 **Eliminated first round**
Group Three: 0–1 vs. Czechoslovakia, 1–0 vs. Mexico, 1–2 vs. Brazil.

1966 **Eliminated first round**
Group Two: 1–2 vs. Argentina, 2–1 vs. Switzerland, 1–2 vs. West Germany.

1978 **Eliminated first round**
Group Three: 1–2 vs. Austria, 0–0 vs. Brazil, 1–0 vs. Sweden.

1982 **Eliminated second round**
Group Five: 1–1 vs. Honduras, 2–1 vs. Yugoslavia, 0–1 vs. Northern Ireland; Group B: 1–2 vs. West Germany, 0–0 vs. England.

1986 **Quarterfinalists**
Group D: 0–1 vs. Brazil, 2–1 vs. Northern Ireland, 3–0 vs. Algeria; Second round: 5–1 vs. Denmark; Quarterfinal: 1–1 vs. Belgium (4–5 on penalties).

1990 **Eliminated second round**
Group E: 0–0 vs. Uruguay, 3–1 vs. South Korea, 2–1 vs. Belgium; Second round: 1–2 vs. Yugoslavia.

• •

SOUTH KOREA

Governing body: Korea Football Association.
Founded: 1928.
Affiliated to FIFA: 1948.
National colors: White shirts, white shorts, white socks.
Manager/Coach: Kim Ho.

South Korea secured one of the two Asian places on offer for the finals after a two-week play-off series held in Qatar. This group contained countries of sharply contrasting cultural and political beliefs, and it is only soccer's unique popularity that could have pitched the Koreas against the Japanese, North against South Korea, and Iraq against Iran. The latter fixture, termed "the mother of all soccer matches," finished 2–1 to Iraq, but it was Iraq's last-minute game-tying goal against the Japanese meant that South Korea had qualified.

The Japanese were probably the best team in the group, and failing to qualify was a big blow for the country that is hoping to host the World Cup finals in 2002.

South Korea's most influential player is likely to be Kim Joo-Sung who, at 28, will be appearing in his third World Cup. He is the only member of the squad playing for a European club, Bochum in Germany. There are also two young players, Seo Jung-won and Noh Jung-yoon (who became South Korea's youngest full international at age 17), who are both very fast and can play anywhere in midfield or in attack.

During the qualifers, South Korea's strategy was to deliver long balls from defense, with rapid movements down both wings. These were often directed to the wingers, who made fast breaks and put in quick crosses to the target men.

South Korea may have picked up some experience from the last two World Cup finals, but they lack the power and penetration to upset the other three teams. Their negative and uninspiring approach to Italia '90 does not bode well for their chances this time, but with more experience they may have improved.

Route to the Finals

Asia: First-round Group D

South Korea	0	Bahrain	0
South Korea	1	Lebanon	0
South Korea	3	India	0
South Korea	3	Hong Kong	0
South Korea	4	Hong Kong	1
South Korea	2	Lebanon	0
South Korea	7	India	0
South Korea	3	Bahrain	0

Played	Won	Drawn	Lost	Goals For	Goals Against	Pts.
8	7	1	0	22	1	15

Second-round

South Korea	3	Iran	0
South Korea	2	Iraq	2
South Korea	1	Saudi Arabia	1
Japan	1	South Korea	0
South Korea	3	North Korea	0

Played	Won	Drawn	Lost	Goals For	Goals Against	Pts.
5	2	2	1	9	4	6

South Korea finished runners-up to Saudi Arabia.

World Cup History

For many years, South Korea has been the most consistent soccer nation in Asia. However, their first appearance on the world stage in 1954 was a daunting one, as they faced the mighty Hungarians, who had not been beaten since 1950. The Koreans were not going to change the order of things and Hungary ran out easy winners. Things didn't get much better in their second game, when Turkey scored seven without reply.

In 1986, the South Koreans became the first Asian team to qualify for two finals and went to Mexico with some optimism. Although they didn't progress beyond the first round, they played attacking soccer and gained their first point from a draw with Bulgaria.

It was a shame that in the following tournament they were defensive and uninspiring. Only against Spain did they show a glimmer of attacking spirit before submitting to sustained Spanish pressure.

Finals appearances: 3 (1954, 1986, 1990).
Biggest win: Has never won.
Biggest defeat: 0–9 vs. Hungary (1954).
Leading scorers: Park Chang-sun, Kim Jong-boo, Choi Soon-ho, Huh Jung-moo, Hwang Bo-kwan (1 goal).

RECORD					
Played	Won	Drawn	Lost	Goals For	Goals Against
8	0	1	7	5	29

● ●

1954   **Eliminated first round**
Group Two: 0–9 vs. Hungary, 0–7 vs. Turkey.
1986   **Eliminated first round**
Group A: 1–3 vs. Argentina, 1–1 vs. Bulgaria,
2–3 vs. Italy.
1990   **Eliminated first round**
Group E: 0–2 vs. Belgium, 1–3 vs. Spain, 0–1
vs. Uruguay.

● ●

GROUP D

ARGENTINA, NIGERIA, BULGARIA, GREECE

Argentina was trounced 5–0 by Colombia during qualification for the finals, but they should justify their seeded status in this group. They will be wary of the African challengers, Nigeria, as it was in the last World Cup tournament that the South Americans, then the champions, lost sensationally to Cameroon in the opening game.

Nigeria represents the best of African football, and their natural flair and athleticism could well make up for their lack of experience at this level. Bulgaria, on the other hand, has a wealth of experience at this level but are harnessed with the unfortunate statistic of having played 16, won 0.

Greece is also making its first appearance in the finals. Although reaching the United States will be considered their main achievement, the team will be guaranteed fanatical support, and opponents will find it difficult to pierce their tight defense.

GROUP D FIXTURES

Argentina vs. Greece	June 21 (Boston)
Nigeria vs. Bulgaria	June 21 (Dallas)
Argentina vs. Nigeria	June 25 (Boston)
Greece vs. Bulgaria	June 26 (Chicago)
Argentina vs. Bulgaria	June 30 (Dallas)
Greece vs. Nigeria	June 30 (Boston)

ARGENTINA

Governing body: *Association del Futbol Argentina.*
Founded: 1893.
Affiliated to FIFA: 1912.

National colors: Light blue-and-white striped shirts, black
shorts, white socks.
Manager/Coach: Alfio Basile.

Because they had reached three of the last four World Cup
finals, winning it twice in the process, it came as something
of a shock to see Argentina struggling through their qualification group in such unconvincing style. A 5–0 drubbing
by Colombia in Buenos Aires put their qualification in
doubt, and they only scraped through to a play-off thanks
to Paraguay's failure to beat Peru in their final match.

Colombia had already beaten Argentina 2–1 in
Barranquilla, a victory that ended Argentina's longest-
ever unbeaten run of 31 internationals. The second loss
was Argentina's worst defeat since 1910 and forced them
into a play-off against the winners of the Oceania group,
Australia, over two games.

In the first game in Sydney, Balbo put Argentina
ahead only for Vidmar to equalize soon after. In Buenos
Aires, a goal by Batistuta gave Argentina the victory,
which ensured they were the last qualifier for USA '94.

The play-off games were somewhat overshadowed by the
return of Diego Maradona. After returning from Europe to
play for Argentinian club team Newell's Old Boys,
Maradona was picked by coach Alfio Basile to captain the
national team. Since then he has been released by his club
and faces criminal charges for firing an air rifle at journalists.
If he does play, Maradona can look forward to his fourth
World Cup, but the big question is what role this controversial player will have. It is easy to recall the Maradona of 1986
and his astonishing contribution to Argentina winning the
World Cup. But he was a shadow of his former self four years
later in Italy. Gone were the surging runs that would take
him powerfully past two or three defenders, and instead he

appeared just an ordinary player on an ordinary team that reached the finals more by good fortune than skill.

Despite struggling to qualify for the World Cup, Argentina gave themselves a boost by winning the 1993 South American Championship. They beat Bolivia and drew with Mexico and Colombia to move into the quarterfinals, where they overcame Brazil after a penalty shootout in which their star goalkeeper of the 1990 World Cup, Goycochea, made the vital stop. He was again the hero when the semifinal against Colombia was also settled on penalties. Argentina had been outplayed in several games but improved to beat Mexico, 2–1, in the final.

Argentina may have to draw inspiration from experienced defender Oscar Ruggeri. Apart from Maradona, the 32-year-old is the sole remaining member of Argentina's 1986 World Cup winning team. He led Argentina to victory in the South American Championship, where he set up Batistuta's goal against Bolivia and scored a timely equalizer against Mexico in the first round. He is popular with many of his teammates, who were openly critical of coach Alfio Basile's decision to make Maradona captain for the games against Australia. They felt Ruggeri was more deserving.

In attack, Batistuta is consistently dangerous but will be closely marked by the opposition. He also played well in the South American Championship and, despite having few opportunities in the final, he managed to break away from defenders to score two excellent goals.

In midfield, Redondo is widely thought of as one of the best players in the game. He reads situations well, and many of Argentina's attacking moves come through him.

There will be plenty of interest in the form of Claudio Caniggia, who will finish his ban for drug abuse only a month before the finals start. But even back to his best, he is unlikely to be able to lift this erratic team single-handedly.

Route to the Finals

South America: Group A

Argentina	1	Peru	0
Argentina	3	Paraguay	1
Colombia	2	Argentina	1
Argentina	2	Peru	1
Argentina	0	Paraguay	0
Argentina	0	Colombia	5

Played	Won	Drawn	Lost	Goals For	Goals Against	Pts.
6	3	1	2	7	9	7

Argentina finished runners-up to Colombia and qualified for the South America/Oceania play-off against Australia.

| Australia | 1 | Argentina | 1 |
| Argentina | 1 | Australia | 0 |

Argentina won 2–1 on aggregate.

World Cup History

Ever since soccer was introduced by the British, Argentina has maintained a proud tradition of producing great players. It was a tragedy that so many of these were persuaded to leave the country and play in Italian and Spanish leagues, leaving the national team below strength for many years. After finishing runners-up to their great rivals Uruguay in the 1930 World Cup final,

Argentina sent a weakened team to Italy, afraid that they would lose more of their star players to the Italian league. As if to prove their point, three Argentinians—Orsi, Guaita, and Monti—played for the World Cup–winning Italian team.

This reason, plus the fact that Argentina was always overlooked as host for the World Cup, meant that it was not until 1958 that they sent another team to the World Cup. Argentina had won the South American Championship the year before with a strong team but again refused to recall their foreign-based players and fielded a weakened side. They were promptly eliminated after the first round.

Argentina was finally awarded the World Cup in 1978 and their manager, Cesar Menotti, built an impressive team to finally take the title. Only Mario Kempes, the tournament's top scorer, played abroad.

Since then, Argentina has been at the forefront of world soccer, appearing in the last two finals, both against West Germany. The side that won in 1986 was more than a one-man team, but there was no denying that Maradona was the inspiration behind a popular success. Four years later the contrast could not have been more marked. Criticized for their negative tactics and reliance on penalty shoot-outs to reach the final, Argentina and a less effective Maradona were beaten by West Germany in one of the poorest finals ever seen.

Finals appearances: 10 (1930, 1934, 1958, 1962, 1966, 1974, 1978, 1982, 1986, 1990).
Biggest win: 6–0 vs. Peru (1978).
Biggest defeat: 1–6 vs. Czechoslovakia (1958).
Leading scorer: Guillermo Stabile (8 goals).

RECORD

Played	Won	Drawn	Lost	Goals For	Goals Against
48	26	7	15	82	59

• •

1930 **RUNNERS-UP**
Group One: 1–0 vs. France, 6–3 vs. Mexico, 3–1 vs. Chile; Semifinal: 6–1 vs. United States; Final: 2–4 vs. Uruguay.

1934 **Eliminated first round**
First round: 2–3 vs. Sweden.

1958 **Eliminated first round**
Group One: 1–3 vs. West Germany, 3–1 vs. Northern Ireland, 1–6 vs. Czechoslovakia.

1962 **Eliminated first round**
Group Four: 1–0 vs. Bulgaria, 1–3 vs. England, 0–0 vs. Hungary.

1966 **Quarterfinalists**
Group Two: 2–1 vs. Spain, 0–0 vs. West Germany, 2–0 vs. Switzerland; Quarterfinal: 0–1 vs. England.

1974 **Eliminated second round**
Group Four: 2–3 vs. Poland; 1–1 vs. Italy, 4–1 vs. Haiti; Group A: 0–4 vs. Holland, 1–2 vs. Brazil, 1–1 vs. East Germany.

1978 **WINNERS**
Group One: 2–1 vs. Hungary, 2–1 vs. France, 0–1 vs. Italy; Group B: 2–0 vs. Poland, 0–0 vs. Brazil, 6–0 vs. Peru; Final: 3–1 vs. Holland.

1982 **Eliminated second round**
Group Three: 0–1 vs. Belgium, 4–1 vs. Hungary, 2–0 vs. El Salvador; Group C: 1–2 vs. Italy, 1–3 vs. Brazil.

1986   **WINNERS**
Group A: 3–1 vs. South Korea, 1–1 vs. Italy, 2–0 vs. Bulgaria; Second round: 1–0 vs. Uruguay; Quarterfinal: 2–1 vs. England; Semifinal: 2–0 vs. Belgium; Final: 3–2 vs. West Germany.

1990   **RUNNERS-UP**
Group B: 0–1 vs. Cameroon, 2–0 vs. Soviet Union, 1–1 vs. Romania; Second round: 1–0 vs. Brazil; Quarterfinal: 0–0 vs. Yugoslavia (3–2 on penalties); Semifinal: 1–1 vs. Italy (4–3 on penalties); Final: 0–1 vs. West Germany.

● ●

NIGERIA

Governing body: Nigeria Football Association.
Founded: 1945.
Affiliated to FIFA: 1959.
National colors: Green shirts, green shorts, green socks.
Manager/Coach: Clemens Westerhof

In recent years, Africa has made impressive progress in world soccer. Cameroon's performance in the 1990 World Cup was recognized as some of the most entertaining soccer in the tournament, and this certainly played a part in FIFA's decision to increase the number of qualifiers from Africa from two to three.

Nigeria is likely to be the strongest of the African qualifers and represents the best in African soccer. The one problem is that they are inexperienced on the world stage, and their uninhibited style could be found out by more experienced teams.

But they are not totally naive. Their football has improved dramatically, as the majority of the team now plays top-level football in the Europe leagues.

Nigeria only qualified on goal difference, ahead of the African champion Ivory Coast, after their final match against Algeria finished 1–1, but they were undoubtedly the best team in their group, beating both of their opponents 4–1 at home.

With eight goals in the qualifers, Rashidi Yekini did more than most to ensure his country's first-ever appearance in the finals. The 1993 African Player of the Year plays for Portuguese club Vitoria Setubal but retains a strong desire to play for his country.

In midfield, 20-year-old Augustine Okocha, who plays for German club Eintrach Frankfurt, is another key player.

It would be a grave error of judgment to take the Nigerians lightly, and although much is expected of the African teams after the triumphs of Cameroon in 1990, Nigeria will live up to their potential.

If any indication is needed that Africa will have a major say in the future of soccer, one need look no farther than last year's World Under-17 tournament held in Japan, where Nigeria beat Ghana in the final.

The Nigerians swept all before them in convincing and exhilarating style—a team dedicated to flowing, attacking football. They scored 20 goals in 6 games, and if they can keep these players together they could be back in eight years' time with a World Cup–winning team!

Route to the Finals

Africa: First-round Group D

Nigeria	4	South Africa	0
Nigeria	1	Congo	0

| Nigeria | 0 | South Africa | 0 |
| Nigeria | 2 | Congo | 0 |

Played	Won	Drawn	Lost	Goals For	Goals Against	Pts.
4	3	1	0	7	0	7

Second-round Group A

Ivory Coast	2	Nigeria	1
Nigeria	4	Algeria	1
Nigeria	4	Ivory Coast	1
Nigeria	1	Algeria	1

Played	Won	Drawn	Lost	Goals For	Goals Against	Pts.
4	2	1	1	10	5	5

World Cup History

Although Nigeria has entered every World Cup since 1962—missing only 1966—this is the first time they have qualified for the finals.

BULGARIA

Governing body: *Bulgsarski Futbolen Soius*.
Founded: 1923.
Affiliated to FIFA: 1924.
National colors: White shirts, green shorts, white socks.
Manager/Coach: Dimitar Penev.

Bulgaria reached their sixth World Cup finals in dramatic style. Requiring victory in Paris against the French in the final match of Group Six, Bulgaria fell a goal behind but staged an astonishing comeback to equalize and then snatch the winner in injury time, both goals being scored by Kostadinov. They were only given this opportunity by an extraordinary finish to France's game against Israel a month earlier. Israel, having lost 4–0 to France in Tel Aviv, produced a shocking reversal, beating them 3–2 with a winner in injury time. France had only needed one point from their last two home games against Israel and Bulgaria to qualify, but had managed to lose both.

Surely Bulgaria can now reverse their unfortunate World Cup finals statistic of having played 16, won 0. They have a team of outstanding individuals, including Hristo Stoichkov, who plays for Barcelona, and Krasimir Balakov, who is a big star in Portugal, where he plays for Sporting Club. Balakov has been little short of sensational at club-level—a midfield dynamo who can create goal-scoring opportunities with incisive passes but who also possesses a ferocious shot that is especially effective from free-kick situations.

This Bulgarian team of top-class individuals is peaking at the right time, but Dimitar Penev, who himself won 90 games for Bulgaria and played in three World Cup finals, has the difficult task of molding the foreign stars together with his home-based players. After their defeat at the hands of Austria during qualification, the Bulgarian press criticized Penev and the foreign players for lack of commitment to the national team. They will need to work collectively; otherwise no amount of star talent will reverse their unfortunate World Cup history.

Route to the Finals

Europe: Group Six

Bulgaria	3	Finland	0
Bulgaria	2	France	0
Sweden	2	Bulgaria	0
Bulgaria	2	Israel	0
Austria	3	Bulgaria	1
Bulgaria	2	Finland	0
Bulgaria	2	Israel	2
Bulgaria	1	Sweden	1
Bulgaria	4	Austria	1
Bulgaria	2	France	1

Played	Won	Drawn	Lost	Goals For	Goals Against	Pts.
10	6	2	2	19	10	1

Bulgaria finished runners-up to Sweden.

World Cup History

Bulgaria played well to qualify for their first World Cup in 1962 at the expense of France, who had finished third four years before. Defeats against Argentina and Hungary and a scoreless draw against England set the pattern for the next three finals. Admittedly, they were up against Brazil, Portugal, and Hungary in 1966, but they fared no better in 1970.

Bulgaria's captain, Bonev was their outstanding player in 1974, and they had chances to beat both Sweden and Uruguay before both games were eventually drawn. Bonev scored against Uruguay, and they were only three minutes away from a first win when Pavoni equalized for the South Americans.

In 1986, Bulgaria did qualify for the second round by virtue of two more drawn games, but they lost tamely to host Mexico.

Finals appearances: 5 (1962, 1966, 1970, 1974, 1986).
Biggest win: Has never won.
Biggest defeat: 1–6 vs. Hungary (1962).
Leading scorer: Christo Bonev (2 goals).

RECORD					
Played	Won	Drawn	Lost	Goals For	Goals Against
16	0	6	10	11	35

● ●

1962 **Eliminated first round**
Group Four: 0–1 vs. Argentina, 1–6 vs. Hungary, 0–0 vs. England.

1966 **Eliminated first round**
Group Three: 0–2 vs. Brazil, 0–3 vs. Portugal, 1–3 vs. Hungary.

1970 **Eliminated first round**
Group Four: 2–3 vs. Peru, 2–5 vs. West Germany, 1–1 vs. Morocco.

1974 **Eliminated first round**
Group Three: 0–0 vs. Sweden, 1–1 vs. Uruguay, 1–4 vs. Holland.

1986 **Eliminated second round**
Group A: 1–1 vs. Italy, 1–1 vs. South Korea, 0–2 vs. Argentina; Second round: 0–2 vs. Mexico.

● ●

GREECE

Governing body: *Elliniki Podosfairiki Omnospondia*.
Founded: 1926.
Affiliated to FIFA: 1927.
National colors: Blue shirts, white shorts, blue socks.
Manager/Coach: Alketas Panagoulias.

The withdrawal of Yugoslavia from Group Five of the European qualifiers gave Greece their best-ever chance of reaching the World Cup finals, with two places being available to just five teams: Russia, Greece, Hungary, Luxembourg, and Iceland.

They started well, with a 1–0 win over Iceland, and the fanatical Greek fans turned out in numbers for their next two games at home against Hungary and Luxembourg. Three points from these matches left Greece requiring only two more points for qualification, which they duly collected with a 1–0 victory over Hungary in Budapest.

After a 1–1 draw with Russia on May 23, 1993, Greece had achieved their dream of qualification. As if to prove that they had qualified by right and not just as a result of the FIFA ban on Yugoslavia, they beat Russia, 1–0, in front of an ecstatic crowd of 55,000 in Athens to finish as impressive winners of their group.

Veteran coach Alketas Panagoulias rejoined the national team last year and has been instrumental in the team's success. He served in the same position between 1971 and 1981 and led Greece to their first and only European Championship finals in 1980. In 1983 he coached in the North American Soccer League and will perhaps be familiar to some Americans as the man who steered the United States squad to the Olympic Games in 1984 and World Cup qualifiers in 1986.

Greece only conceded two goals throughout their qualification games and are the only European team to go through to the finals unbeaten. Their defense is evidently the strong point of the team and will have to prove just as frugal in the United States if they are to progress farther in the tournament.

Greece only conceded two goals, but by the same token they only scored 10 in eight matches (compared to Russia's 15), and their attack is lacking in firepower. They will rely heavily on Panayotis Tsalouhidis being able to support his attacking players with late runs into the penalty area. Tsalouhidis played in all of Greece's qualifying games and is a tough, competitive midfield player who is very dangerous in the air from corners and free kicks.

To strengthen the midfield, Panagoulias recalled veteran Anastassios Mitropoulos, who repaid his manager with goals against Luxembourg and Russia. It was 16 years ago that Mitropoulos made his debut for the national side, and at 36 he will be one of several players over age 30 by the time the finals kick off in June.

Even after the draw for the finals was announced, there was great optimism that Greece would qualify for the second round. This is based on their belief that the top seed, Argentina, will treat them with caution and play too conservatively, while they are very familiar with the strengths and weaknesses of Bulgaria. Nigeria is something of an unknown quantity.

What they can be certain of is the support of the large Greek communities in Chicago and Boston, where they will play all their games. The positive effects of this cannot be underestimated, as good support can lift a team to play above themselves. Greece will also go to the World Cup with a positive attitude that has come from remaining unbeaten throughout their qualifying games. They will certainly be a difficult team to break down.

Route to the Finals

Europe: Group Five

Greece	1	Iceland	0
Greece	1	Iceland	0
Greece	0	Hungary	0
Greece	2	Luxembourg	0
Greece	1	Hungary	0
Greece	1	Russia	1
Greece	3	Luxembourg	1
Greece	1	Russia	0

Played	Won	Drawn	Lost	Goals For	Goals Against	Pts.
8	6	2	0	10	2	1

Greece won Group Five.

World Cup History

Greece has entered every World Cup, apart from 1930 and 1950, although they have never really looked like they qualified for any. However, they have only played regular international fixtures since the early 1970s and did well to qualify for the European Championship in 1980.

GROUP E

ITALY, MEXICO, REPUBLIC OF IRELAND, NORWAY

The Italians must be favorites to win what has been christened "the group of death," but second place is not an easy call. Norway was very impressive in qualifying at England's expense, and the Republic of Ireland has proved that they are a very difficult team to beat. But both European teams may struggle to maintain the high-speed pace of their game in temperatures that will rise to 90 degrees or more. Rather, the conditions might favor the style and tactics of Mexico.

Ireland would have preferred to have played their opening games in Boston, where the large Irish community would have swelled their own traveling supporters. And the dedication of the Irish supporters is legendary. They travel far and wide to urge their team on. The Irish made a lot of friends at the last World Cup in Italy, and in many respects this tournament would be poorer without them. They enjoy being there, experiencing the atmosphere, and this seems to rub off on the players. They may not play the most stylish or technically good football but they play with a passion and get results.

GROUP E FIXTURES

Italy vs. Republic of Ireland	June 18 (New York)
Norway vs. Mexico	June 19 (Washington, D.C.)
Italy vs. Norway	June 23 (New York)
Republic of Ireland vs. Mexico	June 24 (Orlando)
Italy vs. Mexico	June 28 (Washington, D.C.)
Republic of Ireland vs. Norway	June 28 (New York)

ITALY

Governing body: *Federazione Italiana Giuoco Calcio*.
Founded: 1898.
Affiliated to FIFA: 1905.
National colors: Blue shirts, white shorts, blue socks.
Manager/Coach: Arrigo Sacchi.

Italian fans are among the most passionate supporters in the world. Their league is one of the richest and contains more world-class players than any other. Many people fancy the Italians to repeat their success of 1982, and they certainly possess the players to achieve it.

After an uncertain start in qualification, Italy played well when it mattered, winning their final three qualifying matches. Even so, their only really impressive performance was the 3–1 away victory over Portugal, and even in the final game of the group the Italians were given an awful fright as Portugal dominated a game that the Italians had to win to qualify. Toward the end of the game, as the Portuguese were committed to throwing men forward in search of the goal, Dino Baggio finished off an Italian counterattack to win the game and allowed Italy to breathe a collective sigh of relief.

So Italy made it to the finals, but they will have to improve on the inconsistent form they showed throughout the qualifiers. Two defensive errors had presented Switzerland with a 2–0 lead in Cagliari, and it wasn't until seven minutes from time that Roberto Baggio first pulled one back for Italy, leaving Stefano Eranio to score a timely equalizer in the last few seconds.

Throughout the qualification games, it was clear that Baggio was a vital member of the Italian team. He effectively took Italy through the qualifiers with some outstanding individual performances, scoring five goals in the process. Now that Italy has reached the finals, Baggio has the chance to prove he is the best player in the world, and it is hoped that he will make the sort of impression on the competition that Maradona did in 1986. If he lives up to his potential, then Italy will be a serious contender to win their fourth World Cup.

Baggio played in the 1990 World Cup finals shortly after becoming the most expensive striker in the world (he moved from Fiorentina to Juventus for a then world-record fee of $10.25 million). His attacking partnership with Schillaci was a major reason for Italy reaching the semifinals, where they lost to Argentina in a penalty shoot-out.

Since then, Baggio has developed into one of the most creative players in the world. He is a playmaker, midfielder, and striker, and is at his best when allowed the freedom to play to his strengths. From a purely technical point of view it is difficult to find a flaw in his abilities. In recognition of his talent he was named the European Player of the Year and FIFA's World Footballer of the Year for 1993.

But Italy is by no means a one-man team. Alessandro Costacurta partners Franco Baresi in a very experienced defense, and Paolo Maldini must now be one of the most accomplished left-sided defenders in the world. Dino Baggio and Demetrio Albertini support Roberto Baggio in midfield, providing space for him to create scoring opportunities for himself or Giuseppe Signori—the top scorer in the Italian Serie A league. There will also be keen interest in whether Gianlugi Lentini will recover sufficiently from a bad car accident in August 1993 to take part in the finals. Lentini is rated one of the bright-est stars in Italian soccer, a fact illustrated by Milan pay-ing $21 million for his services.

After the scares of qualification, Italy can now settle down to the matter at hand. With fanatical expatriate support, they will be very difficult to beat.

Route to the Finals

Europe: Group One

Italy	2	Switzerland	2
Italy	0	Scotland	0
Italy	2	Malta	1
Italy	3	Portugal	1
Italy	6	Malta	1
Italy	2	Estonia	0
Switzerland	1	Italy	0
Italy	3	Estonia	0
Italy	3	Scotland	1
Italy	1	Portugal	0

Played	Won	Drawn	Lost	Goals For	Goals Against	Pts.
10	7	2	1	22	7	16

Italy won Group 1.

World Cup History

The 1930s were the golden age of Italian football as their great manager, Vittorio Pozzo, guided the national team to consecutive World Cup victories in 1934 and 1938. There was considerable resentment from Argentina, Brazil, and Uruguay that Italy was luring their star players away, and they seemed to have a point when Pozzo fielded three Argentinians who were of Italian extraction.

In 1949, Italy was stunned by the news that the airplane

carrying the brilliant Torino team had crashed into the wall of the Superga Basilica on a hillside near Turin. Every player was killed, including eight of the national team.

Italy sent a team to the 1950 World Cup, but they lost in the first round. There followed another poor display in 1954, and Italy suffered the ultimate disgrace of failing to qualify four years later.

Although they qualified for both the 1962 and 1966 tournaments, performances were still poor, and after a defeat by North Korea the Italian team was greeted by pelted garbage on arrival at the airport.

The decision was made to limit the import of foreign made players in 1964 in the hope that local talent would not be overshadowed. The revival started in 1970, when Italy was unfortunate to come up against probably the finest team ever to play in the World Cup.

But 12 years later the World Cup was Italy's for a third time. After a slow start in the finals, drawing all their opening games, they improved as the tournament progressed with victories over Argentina, Brazil, Poland, and West Germany. The star was Paolo Rossi but it had taken great teamwork to overcome four such worthy opponents.

Finals appearances: 12 (1934, 1938, 1950, 1954, 1962, 1966, 1970, 1974, 1978, 1982, 1986, 1990).
Biggest win: 7–1 vs. United States (1934).
Biggest defeat: 1–4 vs. Switzerland (1954), Brazil (1970).
Leading scorer: Paolo Rossi (9 goals).

RECORD

Played	Won	Drawn	Lost	Goals For	Goals Against
54	31	11	12	89	54

• •

1934   **WINNERS**
First round: 7–1 vs. United States; Second round:
1–1 vs. Spain, 1–0 vs. Spain (replay); Semifinal:
1–0 vs. Austria; Final: 2–1 vs. Czechoslovakia.

1938   **WINNERS**
First round: 2–1 vs. Norway; Second round: 3–1
vs. France; Semifinal: 2–1 vs. Brazil; Final: 4–2
vs. Hungary.

1950   **Eliminated first round**
Group Three: 2–3 vs. Sweden, 2–0 vs. Paraguay.

1954   **Eliminated first round**
Group Four: 1–2 vs. Switzerland, 4–1 vs.
Belgium, 1–4 vs. Switzerland.

1962   **Eliminated first round**
Group Two: 0–0 vs. West Germany, 0–2 vs.
Chile, 3–0 vs. Switzerland.

1966   **Eliminated first round**
Group Four: 2–0 vs. Chile, 0–1 vs. Soviet Union,
0–1 vs. North Korea.

1970   **RUNNERS-UP**
Group Two: 1–0 vs. Sweden, 0–0 vs. Uruguay, 0–0
vs. Israel; Quarterfinal: 4–1 vs. Mexico; Semifinal: 4–3 vs. West Germany; Final: 1–4 vs. Brazil.

1974   **Eliminated first round**
Group Four: 3–1 vs. Haiti, 1–1 vs. Argentina,
1–2 vs. Poland.

1978   **FOURTH PLACE**
Group One: 2–1 vs. France, 3–1 vs. Hungary,
1–0 vs. Argentina; Group A: 0–0 vs. West
Germany, 1–0 vs. Austria, 1–2 vs. Holland;
Third-place play-off: 1–2 vs. Brazil.

1982   **WINNERS**
Group One: 0–0 vs. Poland, 1–1 vs. Peru, 1–1 vs.

Cameroon; Group C: 2–1 vs. Argentina, 3–2 vs. Brazil; Semifinal: 2–0 vs. Poland; Final: 3–1 vs. West Germany.

1986 Eliminated second round

Group A: 1–1 vs. Bulgaria, 1–1 vs. Argentina, 3–2 vs. South Korea; Second round: 0–2 vs. France.

1990 THIRD PLACE

Group A: 1–0 vs. Austria, 1–0 vs. United States, 2–0 vs. Czechoslovakia; Second round: 2–0 vs. Uruguay; Quarterfinal: 1–0 vs. Republic of Ireland; Semifinal: 1–1 vs. Argentina (3–4 on penalties); Third-place play-off: 2-1 vs. England.

● ●

MEXICO

Governing body: *Federacion Mexicana de Futbol Asociación*.
Founded: 1927.
Affiliated to FIFA: 1929.
National colors: Green shirts, white shorts, red socks.
Manager/Coach: Miguel Meija Baron.

Banned from the last World Cup for sneaking overage players into a youth tournament, Mexico qualified well for their ninth World Cup despite a background of problems. Preparations were disrupted by the resignations of two national coaches, which left Miguel

Meija Baron only a short time in which to prepare his squad.

They topped both of their qualifying groups in convincing style as they became the first team, other than the hosts and champions, to qualify for the finals.

With the pressure of qualifying removed, Mexico could relax and was in impressive form in the summer of 1993, winning the CONCACAF Gold Cup and reaching the finals of the South American Championship, where they were competing for the first time as specially invited guests.

Mexico fielded a strong team for the CONCACAF Gold Cup and were in devastating form beating Martinique 9–0 and Canada 8–0, followed by a 1–1 draw against Costa Rica, and more goals in a 6–1 victory over Jamaica. They met the United States in the final in front of a crowd of 120,000 in Aztec Stadium, Mexico City. Although the altitude obviously affected the American players, they were outplayed by the Mexicans who applied relentless pressure, winning 4–0.

Mexico has a number of exciting players and a spectacular if unorthodox goalkeeper. Jorge Campos makes brilliant agility and reflex saves but will also make daring forays to assist in attack.

Campos has top-level experience as a striker and will stand well outside his penalty area when his side is on the offensive. By playing so far upfield he prevents counterattacks—his presence inhibits forwards—but he is also very quick at getting back to his goal area. Obviously this role is fraught with danger, as an attacker can attempt to lob the ball over him, but he also prevents a lot of goals by acting as an extra defender.

The FIFA rule that prevents a goalkeeper picking up the ball if it is played back to him with a teammate's feet (he may pick up a ball headed or chested back to him) favors this style. Most goalkeepers will punt a back pass straight downfield, but Campos welcomes the opportunity to keep possession and set up another attack for his team.

There is no doubt that Mexico is a very useful team, with players of exceptional ability. They have always been an attacking team, but they have now developed defensive solidity and success has added that vital element of confidence. Ambriz is an inspiring captain, Ramon Ramirez a skillful and inventive winger, while up front the tall Luis "Zaguinho" Alves is a powerful player with good dribbling skills and a natural goal-scorer. And Hugo Sanchez will also add experience and flair.

Miguel Meija Baron has built a squad capable of emulating or even bettering their country's best World Cup achievements. They are a well-prepared team who play attacking football. The United States is almost home to them, and they will be guaranteed huge support.

Route to the Finals

CONCACAF: Second-round Group A

Mexico	4	St. Vincent	0
Mexico	2	Honduras	0
Mexico	4	Costa Rica	0
Costa Rica	2	Mexico	0
Mexico	11	St. Vincent	0
Mexico	1	Honduras	1

Played	Won	Drawn	Lost	Goals For	Goals Against	Pts.
6	4	1	1	22	3	9

Final round

El Salvador	2	Mexico	1
Mexico	3	Honduras	0
Mexico	3	El Salvador	1
Mexico	4	Canada	0
Mexico	4	Honduras	1
Mexico	2	Canada	1

Played	Won	Drawn	Lost	Goals For	Goals Against	Pts.
6	5	0	1	17	5	10

Mexico won the group.

World Cup History

Mexico's superiority over their Central American neighbors is illustrated by a fine tradition of qualifying for the World Cup, but they have yet to make a significant mark. It was not until a 3–1 victory over Czechoslovakia in 1962 that Mexico won their first game. Mexico's goalkeeper, Antonio Carbajal, was celebrating his 33d birthday that day, a suitable present for the man who was to play in five consecutive World Cups.

Mexico has twice staged the World Cup, and reaching the quarterfinals in each represents their best finishes. The 1970 team was not especially good, but in 1986, with Sanchez and Nagrette in spectacular goal-scoring form, they only lost out to West Germany in a penalty shoot-out.

Finals appearances: 9 (1930, 1950, 1954, 1958, 1962, 1966, 1970, 1978, 1986).
Biggest win: 4–0 vs. El Salvador (1970).

Biggest defeat: 0–6 vs. West Germany (1978).
Leading scorers: Horacio Casarin, Javier Valdivia Huerta,
  Fernando Quirarte (2 goals).

RECORD

Played	Won	Drawn	Lost	Goals For	Goals Against
29	6	5	18	27	64

• •

1930 **Eliminated first round**
Group One: 1–4 vs. France, 0–3 vs. Chile, 3–6
vs. Argentina.

1950 **Eliminated first round**
Group One: 0–4 vs. Brazil, 1–4 vs. Yugoslavia,
1–2 vs. Switzerland.

1954 **Eliminated first round**
Group One: 0–5 vs. Brazil, 2–3 vs. France.

1958 **Eliminated first round**
Group Three: 0–3 vs. Sweden, 1–1 vs. Wales,
0–4 vs. Hungary.

1962 **Eliminated first round**
Group Three: 0–2 vs. Brazil, 0–1 vs. Spain, 3–1
vs. Czechoslovakia.

1966 **Eliminated first round**
Group One: 1–1 vs. France, 0–2 vs. England,
0–0 vs. Uruguay.

1970 **Quarterfinalists**
Group One: 0–0 vs. Soviet Union, 4–0 vs. El
Salvador, 1–0 vs. Belgium; Quarterfinal: 1–4 vs.
Italy.

1978   **Eliminated first round**
Group Two: 1–3 vs. Tunisia, 0–6 vs. West
Germany, 1–3 vs. Poland.

1986   **Quarterfinalists**
Group B: 2–1 vs. Belgium, 1–1 vs. Paraguay,
1–0 vs. Iraq; Second round: 2–0 vs. Bulgaria;
Quarterfinal: 0–0 vs. West Germany (1–4 on
penalties).

• •

REPUBLIC OF IRELAND

Governing body: The Football Association of Ireland.
Founded: 1921.
Affiliated to FIFA: 1923.
National colors: Green shirts, white shorts, green socks.
Manager/Coach: Jack Charlton.

Under the inspirational management of Jack Charlton,
the Republic of Ireland qualified for their second successive World Cup finals, to the delight of many neutrals.

They came through a very tough qualifying group
which included Denmark, the reigning European champions, and Spain. With victories against the weaker
nations and valuable away draws to Spain and Denmark,
Ireland appeared to be making confident progress. But
just when they needed a solid home game against Spain
they lost control, losing 1–3. This set up a tense final

game against Northern Ireland in Belfast, in which they came from a goal behind to snatch a late equalizer.

In the end, the Republic of Ireland qualified by the smallest margin—finishing joint second with Denmark on points and goal difference—edging out the Danes on goals scored.

Essentially, the key to the team's success is to put the opposition under constant pressure by ensuring the ball stays in their half of the field. They are a team with a never–say–die attitude and will always make things difficult for even the most talented teams: harrying, chasing, and tackling hard. However in the heat and humidity, this tactic will prove energy–sapping.

Manchester United teammates Denis Irwin and Roy Keane have appeared in all of the Republic's World Cup matches and are key members of the team. Keane, Young Player of the Year, has yet to score for his country, but his youth and tireless running will be crucial in helping what is an aging team. Staunton, McGrath, and Houghton also represent one of the English Premier league's top teams, Aston Villa, and their experience playing together at club level will provide valuable understanding.

Despite missing out on playing in Boston, the Republic will still have huge support from expatriates, plus their large traveling contingent. Jack Charlton will once again work his miracles and inspire the team to play above themselves.

Route to the Finals

Europe: Group Three

Republic of Ireland	2	Albania	0
Republic of Ireland	4	Latvia	0
Republic of Ireland	0	Denmark	0

Republic of Ireland	0	Spain	0
Republic of Ireland	3	Northern Ireland	0
Republic of Ireland	1	Denmark	1
Republic of Ireland	2	Albania	1
Republic of Ireland	2	Latvia	0
Republic of Ireland	1	Lithuania	0
Republic of Ireland	2	Lithuania	0
Spain	3	Republic of Ireland	1
Republic of Ireland	1	Northern Ireland	1

Played	Won	Drawn	Lost	Goals For	Goals Against	Pts.
12	7	4	1	19	6	18

Republic of Ireland finished runners-up to Spain in Group Three.

World Cup History

The Republic of Ireland celebrated qualifying for their first finals by reaching the last eight, despite not winning any of their five games. They drew all three opening games against England, Holland, and Morocco, and beat Romania in a tense penalty shoot-out in the second phase. Against the host, Italy, the Republic showed they were capable of attractive soccer, but the day belonged to the new Italian superstar Schillaci, who scored the only goal of the game.

Finals appearances: 1 (1990).
Biggest win: Has only won on penalties.
Biggest defeat: 0–1 vs. Italy (1990).
Leading scorers: Niall Quinn, Kevin Sheedy (1 goal).

<table>
<tr><td colspan="6"><u>RECORD</u></td></tr>
<tr><td>Played</td><td>Won</td><td>Drawn</td><td>Lost</td><td>Goals For</td><td>Goals Against</td></tr>
<tr><td>5</td><td>1</td><td>3</td><td>1</td><td>2</td><td>3</td></tr>
</table>

Played	Won	Drawn	Lost	Goals For	Goals Against
5	1	3	1	2	3

1990   Quarterfinalists
Group F: 1–1 vs. England, 0–0 vs. Egypt, 1–1 vs. Holland; Second round: 0–0 vs. Romania (5–4 on penalties); Quarterfinal: 0–1 vs. Italy.

NORWAY

Governing body: *Norges Fotballforbund Ullevaal Stadion.*
Founded: 1902.
Affiliated to FIFA: 1908.
National colors: Red shirts, white shorts, blue socks.
Manager/Coach: Egil Olsen.

When the qualifying draw of Group Two was announced, most people expected England and Holland to be the two teams traveling to the United States. Norway had other ideas. They ensured their place in America by doing the double over Poland. But the key games took three out of four points off both England and Holland to qualify impressively and sent shock waves around the football world. Losing to Turkey was too late to affect any results.

Norway's success is due to a number of reasons, but most important is coach Egil Olsen. He took over the national team four years ago and by applying his great experience, a systematic approach, and a bit of natural self-belief and enthusiasm, he built up the team's confidence to a level where they truly believe in their ability. Even against the traditional football powers of England, Holland, and Poland, the Norwegians pressurized and harried the opposition in all areas of the field, giving them no time to settle.

With a core of experienced players, Olsen introduced a winning formula and the team has gone from strength to strength, notching up a series of impressive victories.

Good defensive work combined with an enormous amount of running and movement are the main ingredients. The team often plays with just a single attacker, but with five in midfield they maintain a good defense while being very quick to support attacking situations. This style of play does require a lot of movement from the midfielders, and this reliance on work-rate might not stand the heat of the American summer.

The team has no real stars as such, but they work extremely well as a team. There is experience in defense with goalkeeper Erik Thorsvedt and 33-year-old sweeper Rune Bratseth. Bratseth is a cool and poised defender who also poses a serious aerial threat at set pieces. The key men in midfield are Kjetil Rekdal, who scored at Wembley against England, and Erik Mykland, while Jostein Flo's height will be used to unsettle defenders in attack.

Egil Olsen admits that this is a very tough draw, but they had a tough qualifying group and won that. Teamwork is their strength, and they should not be underestimated.

Route to the Finals

Europe: Group 2

Norway	10	San Marino	0
Norway	2	Holland	1

Norway	2	San Marino	0
Norway	1	England	1
Norway	3	Turkey	1
Norway	2	England	0
Norway	0	Holland	0
Norway	1	Poland	0
Norway	3	Poland	0
Turkey	2	Norway	1

Played	Won	Drawn	Lost	Goals For	Goals Against	Pts.
10	7	2	1	25	5	16

Norway won Group Two.

World Cup History

Qualification for the 1938 World Cup represents the only occasion that Norway has been present in the finals, and they were unfortunate to draw world champion Italy, in their first game. The Norwegian amateurs took the champions to extra time, but ended up losing 2–1.

Finals appearances: 1 (1938).
Biggest win: Has never won.
Biggest defeat: 1–2 vs. Italy (1938).
Leading scorer: Arne Brustad (1 goal).

RECORD					
Played	Won	Drawn	Lost	Goals For	Goals Against
1	0	0	1	1	2

● ●

1938 **Eliminated first round**
First round: 1–2 vs. Italy.

● ●

GROUP F

BELGIUM, HOLLAND, MOROCCO, SAUDI ARABIA

Belgium, as top seed, will have to play above themselves to beat Holland who could go a long way in the tournament. Both should qualify for the second phase comfortably. Morocco is developing into a useful team but it is difficult to see Saudi Arabia winning a game.

GROUP F FIXTURES

Belgium vs. Morocco	June 19 (Orlando)
Holland vs. Saudi Arabia	June 20 (Washington, D.C.)
Belgium vs. Holland	June 25 (Orlando)
Morocco vs. Saudi Arabia	June 25 (New York)
Belgium vs. Saudi Arabia	June 29 (Washington, D.C.)
Morocco vs. Holland	June 29 (Orlando)

BELGIUM

Governing body: *Union Royale Belge des Societes de Football-Association.*
Founded: 1895.
Affiliated to FIFA: 1904.
National colors: Red shirts, red shorts, red socks.
Manager/Coach: Paul van Himst.

After being overshadowed by their Dutch neighbors in the 1970s, Belgian soccer has earned a highly respected place on the world map in the last decade. Clubs like Bruges, Mechelen, and Anderlecht all have won European honors and the national team reached the semifinals of the World Cup in Mexico in 1986, losing to Argentina.

In what appeared to be a competitive group, all seemed to be going smoothly for Belgium in their bid to qualify for their eighth World Cup finals. However, after building a huge early lead with six straight victories in Group Four, they struggled through by taking just three points from their last four matches, and qualification looked decidedly nervous at the end.

Much of the Belgian team is built around a core of experienced players, and as such they will be one of the best-organized of the European challengers.

In defense, Georges Grun and Philippe Albert form a formidable partnership, backed by the continued brilliance of veteran goalkeeper Michel Preud'homme. In midfield, Franky van der Elst and Lorenzo Staelens support Enzo Scifo, a brilliant playmaker and scorer of spectacular goals. Scifo is the biggest star of the Belgian team, and they rely on him to provide a spark of genius.

In attack, Brazilian-born Luis Oliveira is an experienced and effective striker and Luc Nilis has shown that he is one of the most technically gifted strikers around. He is a regular scorer for his club, though he has yet to score for his country. Marc Wilmots is another player with potential, while coach Paul van Himst gave veteran Alex Czerniatynski a call-up for the crucial qualifer against Czechoslovakia. He scored the winner to stake his claim for the trip to the United States.

Solid in defense, industrious, and creative in midfield, Belgium need to find a consistent striker to complete a useful-looking team. Many Belgians hope that Croat-born Josip Weber will be that man and that he will be granted citizenship in time to represent Belgium in the finals.

Route to the Finals

Europe: Group Four

Belgium	1	Cyprus	0
Belgium	3	Faroe Islands	0
Belgium	2	Czechoslovakia	1
Belgium	1	Romania	0
Belgium	2	Wales	0
Belgium	3	Cyprus	0
Wales	2	Belgium	0
Belgium	3	Faroe Islands	0
Romania	2	Belgium	1
Belgium	0	Czechoslovakia	0

Played	Won	Drawn	Lost	Goals For	Goals Against	Pts.
10	7	1	2	16	5	15

Belgium finished runners-up to Romania.

World Cup History

Belgium, a founding member of FIFA, made little impression on soccer's world stage until the 1970s. As players moved from semiprofessional to professional status, the standard at club level improved to such an extent that Anderlecht won the European Winners Cup in 1976.

The national team was runner-up to West Germany in the 1980 European Championship and qualified for the World Cup two years later. But the team's greatest achievement came in the 1986 finals, when they were beaten by Argentina in the semifinals. They had beaten the Soviet Union and Spain on the way, and the difference between the teams was one Diego Maradona, who scored two tremendous goals.

Finals appearances: 8 (1930, 1934, 1938, 1954, 1970, 1986, 1990).
Biggest win: 4–3 vs. Soviet Union (1986).
Biggest defeat: 2–5 vs. Germany (1934).
Leading scorer: Jan Ceulemans (4 goals).

RECORD					
Played	Won	Drawn	Lost	Goals For	Goals Against
25	8	3	14	33	49

● ●

1930 **Eliminated first round**
Group Four: 0–3 vs. United States, 0–1 vs. Paraguay.

1934 **Eliminated first round**
First round: 2–5 vs. Germany.

1938 **Eliminated first round**
First round: 1–3 vs. France.

1954 **Eliminated first round**
Group Four: 4–4 vs. England, 1–4 vs. Italy.

1970 **Eliminated first round**
Group One: 3–0 vs. El Salvador, 1–4 vs. Soviet Union, 0–1 vs. Mexico.

1982 **Eliminated second round**
Group Three: 1–0 vs. Argentina, 1–0 vs. El Salvador, 1–1 vs. Hungary; Group A: 0–3 vs. Poland, 0–1 vs. Soviet Union.

1986 **FOURTH PLACE**
Group B: 1–2 vs. Mexico, 2–1 vs. Iraq, 2–2 vs. Paraguay; Second round: 4–3 vs. Soviet Union; Quarterfinal: 1–1 vs. Spain (5–4 on penalties); Semifinal: 0–2 vs. Argentina; Third-place play-off: 2–4 vs. France

1990   **Eliminated second round**
Group E: 2–0 vs. South Korea, 3–1 vs. Uruguay,
1–2 vs. Spain; Second round: 0–1 vs. England.

• •

HOLLAND

Governing body: *Koninklijke Nederlandsche Voetbalbond.*
Founded: 1889.
Affiliated to FIFA: 1904.
National colors: Orange shirts, white shorts, orange socks.
Manager/Coach: Dick Advocaat.

The Dutch let themselves down in 1990. They were considered one of the strongest teams in the world, but inter-
nal squabbling resulted in average performances and an
early exit, albeit to West Germany. Much will depend on
the individual talents of the players gelling to the collective good this time.

Holland made up for a poor start in their qualifying
group with decisive victories at home over England and
away over Poland, to take the second qualifying place
behind Norway. The Scandinavians had taken the
expected qualifiers, England and Holland, by surprise
with victories over both in Norway. Hence, the remaining place would be decided between Holland and
England in Rotterdam.

In this game Ronald Koeman was lucky to still be on
the field after deliberately bringing down David Platt

when it seemed the Englishman would score. Not only did Koeman avoid being sent off, he went on to rub salt into England's wound by scoring from a free kick shortly afterward. The Dutch could not afford to relax until Dennis Bergkamp put the game beyond reach six minutes later.

Dennis Bergkamp is one of the rising stars of European football and a man whose attacking skill will be relied upon more than ever now that Marco van Basten has been ruled out of the finals through injury. Bergkamp is the natural successor to players like van Basten and Johann Cruyff, and was brought up through the same youth teams at Ajax. It was Cruyff who recognized Bergkamp's talent when he was technical director at Ajax, and gave Bergkamp his first senior game. He developed quickly, and in 1991 became joint top scorer in the Dutch league, along with the Brazilian Romario. He was out on his own the following season and started to attract the attention of the big Italian clubs.

He is certainly a player who can rise to the big occasion. He scored five times during the qualifiers, including two crucial and clinically taken goals against England. In summer 1993 he moved to Inter Milan for $12 million.

Others to watch in the Dutch squad are Barcelona's Ronald Koeman, who may be lacking pace these days but still possesses one of the most powerful shots in soccer, and is devastating at free kicks.

Speed is something that Marc Overmars has to burn. He scored within five minutes of his debut against Turkey, and his acceleration against England at Wembley forced England's Des Walker, who is no slouch, to concede a vital penalty. The task of taking that penalty fell to Peter van Vossen, who cooly converted the kick to take his tally to six.

Ruud Gullit will be adding his considerable talent to the team after having talks with Dick Advocaat. Gullit has really been turning it on for his Italian club Sampdoria, but he was openly critical of Advocaat's tactics after Holland's 2–2 draw against England.

It was generally accepted that once Holland had qualified for the finals, Johann Cruyff would take over as manager of the national team, replacing Advocaat. Gullit stated that he would rejoin the national team once Cruyff was manager, but in a dramatic revelation Advocaat was offered the job of leading Holland at the finals. A failure to agree on terms between the Dutch FA and Cruyff was suggested as a reason for the split, but family concerns about Cruyff's health were also thought to be contributing factors. But it is a fair reward for Advocaat having got Holland to the finals, and he is someone who will make the Dutch fight all the way.

Route to the Finals

Europe: Group Two

Norway	2	Holland	1
Holland	2	Poland	2
Holland	3	Turkey	1
Holland	3	Turkey	1
Holland	6	San Marino	0
Holland	2	England	2
Holland	0	Norway	0
Holland	7	San Marino	0
Holland	2	England	0
Holland	3	Poland	1

Holland finished runners-up to Norway in Group Two.

Played	Won	Drawn	Lost	Goals For	Goals Against	Pts.
10	6	3	1	29	9	15

World Cup History

Dutch soccer blossomed spectacularly in the early 1970s. After years of Dutch non-qualification for the World Cup, the introduction of a professional league system revolutionized the club structure and saw the rise of the big clubs: Feyenoord, PSV Eindhoven, and Ajax. Feyenoord won the 1970 European Cup only for Ajax to win it for the next three years and become the dominant club in Europe. The Ajax team consisted of some of the best players to come out of Holland: Neeskens, Krol, Rep, Haan. And with Johann Cruyff, they perhaps had the best player in the world.

They formed the basis of the national team that so nearly won the 1974 World Cup. The team played total football: Each skillful player could play in most positions on the field and was totally comfortable with the ball. It produced some of the most exciting football ever seen.

Cruyff refused to go to Argentina for the 1978 finals. Had he gone, Holland could well have beaten the Argentians, who were desperate for success in front of their home support. As it was they came close to winning in the last minute when Rensenbrink hit the post, but Mario Kempes struck for Argentina in extra time.

Finals appearances: 5 (1934, 1938, 1974, 1978, 1990).
Biggest win: 5–1 vs. Austria (1978).
Biggest defeat: 0–3 vs. Czechoslovakia (1938).
Leading scorer: Johannes Rep (7 goals).

RECORD

Played	Won	Drawn	Lost	Goals For	Goals Against
20	8	6	6	35	23

• •

1934 **Eliminated first round**
First round: 2–3 vs. Switzerland.

1938 **Eliminated first round**
First round: 0–3 vs. Czechoslovakia.

1974 **RUNNERS-UP**
Group Three: 2–0 vs. Uruguay, 0–0 vs. Sweden, 4–1 vs. Bulgaria; Group A: 4–0 vs. Argentina, 2–0 vs. East Germany, 2–0 vs. Brazil; Final: 1–2 vs. West Germany.

1978 **RUNNERS-UP**
Group Four: 3–0 vs. Iran, 0–0 vs. Peru, 2–3 vs. Scotland; Group A: 5–1 vs. Austria, 2–2 vs. West Germany, 2–1 vs. Italy; Final: 1–3 vs. Argentina.

1990 **Eliminated second round**
Group F: 1–1 vs. Egypt, 0–0 vs. England, 1–1 vs. Republic of Ireland, Second round: 1–2 vs. West Germany.

• •

MOROCCO

Governing body: *Federation Royale Marocaine de Football.*
Founded: 1955.
Affiliated to FIFA: 1956.
National colors: Red shirts, red shorts, red socks.
Manager/Coach: Abdellah Blinda.

Morocco booked their passage to the United States with a controversial 1–0 victory over Zambia, but their most impressive performance came when they beat Senegal 3–1 in Dakar.

The dramatic finale came at the Mohammed V Stadium in Casablanca, where Zambia needed only a draw to qualify above the Moroccans. The Zambian team, rebuilt after a tragic air crash that had killed 18 players, were favorites to pull off the draw. The atmosphere was tense following protests about the Gabonese referee (Zambia and Gabon were at diplomatic loggerheads over the official investigation into the accident), but there was no quarrel with the Moroccan goal. In a desperate search for the tying goal Zambia pushed forward and was denied a penalty early in the second half. Morocco had demonstrated a well-organized defense, and held out to win the game.

Morocco conceded only four goals in qualification, and much of the credit was due to Nourredine Naybet, their talented sweeper. He now plays in France, as does their top scorer, Mohammed Chaouch.

Route to the Finals

Africa: First-round Group F

Morocco	5	Ethiopia	0
Morocco	1	Benin	0

Morocco	1	Tunisia	1
Morocco	1	Ethiopia	0
Morocco	5	Benin	0
Morocco	0	Tunisia	0

Played	Won	Drawn	Lost	Goals For	Goals Against	Pts.
6	4	2	0	13	1	10

Second-round Group B

Morocco	1	Senegal	0
Zambia	2	Morocco	1
Morocco	3	Senegal	1
Morocco	1	Zambia	0

Played	Won	Drawn	Lost	Goals For	Goals Against	Pts.
4	3	0	1	6	3	6

World Cup History

Ever since they gave West Germany a scare in 1970, no one has underestimated the Moroccans. In 1986 they held England and Poland to a draw, and only lost 1–0 to West Germany in the second round.

Finals appearances: 2 (1970, 1986).
Biggest win: 3–1 vs. Portugal (1986).
Biggest defeat: 0–3 vs. Peru (1970).
Leading scorer: Abdelrazak Khairi (2 goals).

RECORD

Played	Won	Drawn	Lost	Goals For	Goals Against
7	1	3	3	5	8

• •

1970 **Eliminated first round**
Group Four: 1–2 vs. West Germany, 0–3 vs. Peru, 1–1 vs. Bulgaria.

1986 **Eliminated second round**
Group F: 0–0 vs. Poland, 0–0 vs. England, 3–1 vs. Portugal; Second round: 0–1 vs. West Germany.

• •

SAUDI ARABIA

Governing body: Saudi Arabian Football Federation.
Founded: 1959.
Affiliated to FIFA: 1959.
National colors: White shirts, green shorts, white socks.
Manager/Coach: Jorge Solari.

Saudi Arabia makes the trip to the United States on the back of an unbeaten record throughout their qualification campaign and finishing on top of the final group in Qatar after defeating Iran 4–3 in their last game.

One of the best individual performances came from Khalid Al Muwallid, a promising 21–year-old who showed some excellent touches in midfield and scored a fine winning goal against North Korea, while Saeed Owairran scored seven goals in Saudi's qualification.

The team will want for nothing during their preparation for the finals, thanks to the huge financial support provided by the Saudi royal family. However, they will struggle to buck the trend, and will follow the path of all previous Middle Eastern qualifers and fail to reach the second round.

Egypt only lost once in 1990, shutting up shop against the Republic of Ireland and Holland, and narrowly losing to England; Iraq never lost by more than one goal four years earlier. Kuwait provided some comedy in 1982.

Newly appointed Dutch coach Leo Beenhakker, who coached Holland in the 1990 finals, was fired only three months into the job as players objected to his training methods and style of play. His assistant, Wim Jansen, is also returning to Holland. The new coach, Jorge Solari, will be hard-pressed to build a competitive squad in only three months.

Route to the Finals

Asia: First round Group E

Saudi Arabia	6	Macao	0
Saudi Arabia	1	Malaysia	1
Saudi Arabia	0	Kuwait	0
Saudi Arabia	8	Macao	0
Saudi Arabia	3	Malaysia ·	0
Saudi Arabia	2	Kuwait	0

Played	Won	Drawn	Lost	Goals For	Goals Against	Pts.
6	4	2	0	20	1	10

Second round

Saudi Arabia	0	Japan	0
Saudi Arabia	2	North Korea	1
Saudi Arabia	1	South Korea	1
Saudi Arabia	1	Iraq	1
Saudi Arabia	4	Iran	3

Played	Won	Drawn	Lost	Goals For	Goals Against	Pts.
5	2	3	0	8	6	7

Saudi Arabia won their final group.

ALL-TIME GREATS

The true stars of every World Cup are the players. No one forgets the important role of the officials, spectators, and managers, but it is the players who are the true heroes, and their actions are the ones that will be consigned to memory. Not all are prolific goal scorers. Soccer is a team game, and some of the most memorable performances have come from goalkeepers and defenders. In this chapter we look at some of the true greats of World Cup soccer.

FRANZ BECKENBAUER

Franz Beckenbauer was an outstanding captain and supreme attacking sweeper. Born in Munich in 1945, he was playing for Bayern Munich before he was 18 and had established himself as a regular member of the national side by the age of 20. He was something of an introvert and was known as "Der Kaiser" for his supposed arrogance, when, in fact, he was a shy and pleasant man.

In the 1966 World Cup Beckenbauer scored twice against Switzerland in his first World Cup game and also found the net against Uruguay and the Soviet Union. In the final, Beckenbauer played much deeper in defense to mark England's Bobby Charlton, and although he kept the England forward quiet, West Germany lacked the creative touches in midfield that Beckenbauer normally provided. England won, 4–2, in a memorable match.

In the 1970 World Cup, the two teams met again in the quarterfinals. Beckenbauer had now developed his role as an attacking sweeper, where his ability to read the game was crucial to West Germany's success. England took a 2–0 lead, and it was Beckenbauer again who orchestrated the Germans' recovery and subsequent victory.

Beckenbauer led a great West German team to the 1972 European Championship and was named European Footballer of the Year, a title he was awarded again in 1976. But his greatest triumph came in 1974, when he captained West Germany to a 2–1 victory over Holland in the World Cup final.

He retired from international soccer in 1977 after winning 103 games for his country, but soon joined the New York Cosmos where he won two North American Soccer League championships. He was appointed national coach in 1984 and took West Germany to the 1986 and 1990 World Cup finals, becoming only the second man to win the World Cup as a player and manager when West Germany beat Argentina in the 1990 final.

PELE

He was born Edson Arantes do Nascimento, but to soccer fans all over the world he is known as Pele. Born in 1940 in Tres Coracoes, Brazil, he went on to become the greatest player of all time.

Amazingly, Pele played for just two clubs throughout his career. A natural athlete, he excelled at soccer and made his senior debut for his beloved Santos when he was only 15. He made his international debut at the age of 16 in 1957, coming on as a substitute against Argentina and scoring.

Pele missed the first two games of the 1958 World Cup before making his World Cup debut against Russia. He scored his first World Cup goal against Wales, scored a hat trick against France in the semifinal, and completed his World Cup scoring with two more in Brazil's 5–2 win over Sweden in the final.

Injury in the second game of the 1962 World Cup prevented Pele from taking any further part in the competition, and ruthless tackling in a game against Portugal four years later led to Pele threatening never to play in the World Cup again.

But before the 1970 triumph came the little matter of scoring his 1000th goal in November 1969 against Vasco de Gama at the Maracana in Rio. Despite Pele's incredible scoring record, he was quick to create the opportunity for others. In the 1970 World Cup final he headed Brazil into the lead before setting up Jairzinho and then Carlos Alberto with wonderful passes. Throughout the competition, Pele demonstrated a wonderful range of skills, the most outrageous example probably being a lob from his own half against Czechoslovakia that missed the goal by inches.

Pele played his final game for Santos in 1974, but came out of retirement to join his second club, the New York Cosmos. He played his farewell game for the Cosmos in front of a crowd of 75,000 in 1977.

The mark that Pele has left on world football is immeasurable. He became the name by which greatness is measured. His goal-scoring achievements were staggering, and his great enthusiasm for the game should be a lesson for all. He is still an ambassador for the game.

JOHAN CRUYFF

Cruyff was one of the outstanding players of the 70s and one of the greatest all–around players the world has seen. Tall, yet slightly built, Cruyff had stunning acceleration and the ability to change direction instantly. His speed was deceptive, but his excellent control was there for all to see. Perhaps his only failing was his demonstrative temperament.

Cruyff was born in a poor district of Amsterdam in 1947. His mother worked as a cleaner at Ajax, the club with which Cruyff would bring so much success, but, in 1947, soccer in Holland was played largely on an amateur or semiprofessional basis. By 1970, Holland had grown to be one of the most successful countries in Europe.

At the tender age of 10 years, the young Cruyff was playing in the Ajax youth scheme (one that has seen the development of many of today's stars, like Van Basten and Bergkamp). He made his debut for the first team at the age of 17 and helped Ajax win the championship in only his second season. Then followed the League and Cup double as Cruyff became top goal scorer in the Dutch league. Cruyff won his first international cap at the age of 19 against Hungary and steered Ajax, his club side, to three consecutive European Cup victories from 1971 to 1973.

Following this phenomenal success many European teams were keen to sign the Dutch star, and in 1973 Cruyff joined Barcelona for a record fee of $1,383,000. Later that year, he was voted European Footballer of the Year for the second time.

Holland qualified for the 1974 World Cup in Germany, and Cruyff more than anyone orchestrated their progress to the final, where they lost to the hosts. However, their fluid style of play known as "total football" impressed the world.

Cruyff helped Holland reach the 1978 World Cup finals, but refused to go to Argentina for the finals. He was only 31 and could perhaps have swung the balance for Holland, but one can only respect his motives.

He subsequently came out of retirement and spent three years in the NASL before returning to Spain in 1981 to play for Levante. However, the following year he returned to Ajax, winning another league title with them and another with Feyenoord, whom he joined in 1984.

He led Ajax to the European Cup Winners Cup as manager in 1987 and joined Barcelona as manager and led them to two Spanish Cup wins and a European Cup Winners Cup success.

He scored 33 goals in 48 internationals for Holland. He also scored 287 goals in Holland and the United States, and was named European Footballer of the Year three times.

DIEGO MARADONA

The boy wonder, Diego Armand Maradona, was born in Buenos Aires on October 30, 1960 to a poor family. He showed exceptional ability at an early age, and made his senior debut for Argentinos Juniors 10 days before his 16th birthday. In February of his second season he became Argentina's youngest-ever international at 16, when he was selected to play against Hungary.

Such was his talent that the Argentinian coach Luis Cesar Menotti was worried that the youngster would suffer as a result of the pressure and attention, particularly in the buildup to the World Cup, which Argentina was hosting. Menotti made the brave and unpopular decision to leave him out of the squad for the finals. Luckily for Menotti, Argentina won the World Cup.

Maradona was in outstanding goal-scoring form for his club and was signed by Boca Juniors in 1980. He then joined Barcelona for a then world-record fee of nearly $7.5 million in 1982.

His reputation in world soccer had reached such a height that when he appeared for his country in the 1982 World Cup finals in Spain he was a marked man. He made his World Cup debut on his new home ground, the Nou Camp stadium in Barcelona, but was subjected to some rough tactics. However, he scored twice against Hungary as Argentina got through to the second round. Against Italy he faced the experienced defender, Gentile, who followed Maradona all over the pitch, chopping him down time and again. Maradona took his frustration out on Brazil in the next game and was sent off for kicking out at Batista. His and Argentina's tournament was over.

Maradona brought success to Barcelona, but in the summer of 1986 he joined Napoli for another record fee of $10.34 million. But this summer was to be Maradona's greatest. This time the World Cup was held in Mexico, and the Argentinian was now at the peak of his career.

In the opening game he was involved in all three goals against South Korea, and this set the scene for the rest of the tournament. Although a marked man, he was stronger, quicker, and more mature—he took the knocks, but most of the time defenders were chasing his shadow. He made a good Argentinian team into an excellent one, and against England and Belgium scored two of the most memorable goals in the history of the World Cup.

Maradona helped Napoli to the League and Cup double in 1987; they repeated their League success in 1990. In the World Cup of that year, Maradona was no longer the force he had been although he captained Argentina to the final. Since then Maradona's career has been, plagued by injury, drug scandals, and constant pressure from the media.

GERD MULLER

Gerd Muller was a striker with an instinctive feel for scoring goals. Nicknamed "Der Bomber," he may not have scored spectacular goals from 25 yards, but once inside the penalty area he always seemed to be quickest to react to the opportunity, quickest to the ball, and lethal in his execution.

Born in November 1945 in Bavaria, Muller began playing for his local club, Nordlingen, before joining Bayern Munich, who signed another talented youngster, Franz Beckenbauer, around the same time. With the great Sepp Maier in goal, Bayern Munich started out on the most successful phase of its history. German Cup victory in 1966 and 1967 and European Cup Winners Cup success, also in 1967, were followed by the Bundesliga title as German champions in the 1968–69 season. Throughout this time, Muller was scoring at a prolific rate.

Muller made his national team debut in 1966 in West Germany's first game after their World Cup final defeat. By 1970 he was averaging a goal a game and helped West Germany reach the World Cup finals, where they were one of the favorites to win. He scored in their 2–1 victory over Morocco and announced his presence in true style with successive hat tricks against Bulgaria and Peru to set up a repeat quarterfinal encounter against England, winners of the 1966 final. England took a 2–0 lead, but the Germans levelled the score before Muller volleyed the winner. In the semifinal against Italy, Muller scored two more to take his total for the tournament to 10, but it was not enough to stop the Italians going through 4–3. Recognition of his performances followed, as he was voted European Footballer of the Year.

Bayern Munich continued to dominate the Bundesliga, with Muller as West Germany's leading league scorer for three successive years. In 1974, West Germany reached the World Cup final to face Holland. With the score at 1–1, Muller received the ball in the area and scored with a brilliant goal on the turn that left Krol, the Dutch defender, struggling to keep his balance. It was only a half-chance, but demonstrated the striker's instinct and characterized Muller's style. He would spend hours in practice making darting runs and quick turns, confident that he could turn quicker than big defenders.

This World Cup–winning goal took Muller's total to a record aggregate of 14 in World Cup finals and marked his last match in international football. He had scored 68 goals in 62 internationals. His tally of goals in the Bundesliga was 365, and he scored 36 goals in the European Cup—Europe's toughest club competition.

JUAN ALBERTO SCHIAFFINO

Juan Alberto Schiaffino masterminded the Uruguayan team in two World Cups and confounded the critics who had claimed that with his slight physique he would be no match for the toughest defenders. He became one of the best attacking players of his generation.

Born in Montevideo in 1925, Schiaffino joined the

Penarol youth team at 17 and quickly earned his place on the first team. The slender Schiaffino was a fine passer of the ball and demonstrated great vision. He was quick, had excellent control, and was a superb finisher.

Schiaffino was selected for the national team, and in the 1950 World Cup finals Uruguay faced only Bolivia in their group. Schiaffino scored four in a runaway 8–0 success that put them into the final pool against Brazil, Sweden, and Spain.

After a desperate 2–2 draw against Spain and coming from behind twice to beat Sweden 3–2, Uruguay was set to face the overwhelming favorites, Brazil, in the Maracana stadium. It seemed a formality for the hosts, and they piled continuous pressure on Uruguay, eventually scoring two minutes inside the second half. But Uruguay was a spirited side and determined not to let Brazil settle. Schiaffino worked tirelessly throughout, and his efforts were rewarded with an equalizer in the 66th minute. Schiaffino then instigated another move for Ghiggia to score. Unbelievably, Uruguay had won, and they were given a heroes' welcome when they returned to Montevideo.

Four years later, Schiaffino was part of a talented Uruguayan team that beat Scotland 7–0 and England 4–2 on the way to the semifinals. Here, they met the mighty Hungarians, but despite going two goals down Uruguay again showed great resilience to equalize and force the game into extra time. Both Uruguayan goals came from Hohberg, but it was Schiaffino who created both chances. In extra time, Schiaffino was injured, which allowed Hungary to regain their advantage.

Schiaffino was now at the height of his career, and shortly after the 1954 World Cup finals, AC Milan paid a world-record fee of approximately $108,000 for him. Schiaffino enjoyed a long career in Italy before retiring in 1962.

In 1976, Schiaffino took charge of his old club Penarol and even had a brief tenure as the national team manager.

GORDON BANKS

Gordon Banks rivals Russia's Lev Yashin as the greatest goalkeeper ever to play in the World Cup. And if he is remembered for just one incident, it must surely be the one-handed save he made on Pele in the 1970 World Cup. Pele met Jaiizinho's cross with a powerful downward header that seemed certain to be a goal. But Banks flung himself to his right and managed to scrape the ball off the line and send it upwards over the crossbar in what is still considered the finest reaction save ever made.

Born in Sheffield in 1937, Banks signed first for Chesterfield and, after finishing his national service, he signed for Leicester City in 1959. He made his international debut in 1963 against old enemy Scotland who, ironically, were to be the opposition in his last international match nine years and 73 caps later.

Banks was an agile and brave goalkeeper and quickly established himself as first choice for England. He had great positional sense and natural elasticity. At his peak, Banks was regarded as the greatest goalkeeper in the world; yet he never played for a fashionable club.

In the 1966 World Cup, he remained unbeaten in England's first four games, and it was not until the semifinal that Eusebio managed to put the ball past him—and that was one from the penalty spot. For sheer drama, the final was one of history's finest, but Banks and England achieved their dream.

England arrived in Mexico for the 1970 World Cup finals with a stronger squad than the one that had won the cup four years before. Banks was still keeping all at bay, but England looked shaky in their opening game against Romania, despite winning 1–0. Then followed the game that would have proved a fitting final. Brazil, with Pele, Jairzinho, Rivelino, and Tostao, was a formidable side, but England matched them in every department. Banks could do nothing to stop Jairzinho's drive, but his save from Pele's header kept England in the match.

Despite this loss, victory over Czechoslovakia set up a quarterfinal clash against West Germany. Two days before the game, Banks learned that he was to be awarded the Order of the British Empire (OBE), but on the morning of the game he was taken ill with a stomach ailment and was unfit to play. England should still have won as they took a 2–0 lead, but errors from the replacement goalkeeper and a tactical mistake of bringing off Bobby Charlton rather than the tiring Terry Cooper allowed the Germans to win the game 3–2.

At the beginning of the 1972–73 season, Banks was involved in a car crash and suffered serious damage to his right eye that effectively finished his career, although he had two seasons with Fort Lauderdale in 1977–78.

EUSEBIO

Eusebio was a vital ingredient in the success of Portuguese football at both the club and international level throughout the 1960s.

Born in Mozambique in 1942, Eusebio da Silva Ferreira was a supreme artist with the ball and was gifted with superb athleticism. At the age of 19, he moved from his local club to join Benfica of Lisbon. He quickly established himself as a lethal striker, scoring twice in Benfica's 5–3 defeat of the mighty Real Madrid in the 1962 European Cup final.

Eusebio won the first of his international caps for Portugal in 1961 and was voted European Footballer of the Year the same year, an honor he was to receive again in 1965.

His brilliant performances and stunning goals in the 1966 World Cup made him the tournament's top scorer with nine goals—four coming in the amazing fightback against North Korea. Although no one man is greater than the team, Eusebio proved himself the exception in this extraordinary game. The North Koreans had already sent Italy to an ignominious defeat, and within 25 minutes of their quarterfinal against Portugal, one of the cup favorites, they were 3–0 up. Eusebio refused to accept defeat and almost singlehandedly dragged his team back into contention with two goals before halftime. After an hour he equalized, then scored a fourth before Augusto completed Portugal's 5–3 victory.

It was to be a different story in the semifinals, as England's well–organized team prevented Eusebio the opportunity of making his usual impression. Perhaps the most abiding memory is of a distraught Eusebio being comforted by teammates after their 2–1 loss to the eventual champions.

Eusebio will be best remembered for his tremendous speed and one of the most ferocious right-foot shots seen. He was the top scorer in the Portuguese league every year from 1964 to 1973 and helped Benfica to considerable domestic and European success.

A knee injury in the 1970s effectively finished his first-class career, although he reappeared in Mexico and the United States, and in 1976 helped Toronto Metros-Croatia with the Soccer Bowl.

BOBBY CHARLTON

Bobby Charlton possessed a sublime talent on the pitch throughout his playing career and continues to be a wonderful ambassador for the game to this day.

Born in 1937, Charlton signed for Manchester United in 1954 as one of United's Busby Babes, the nickname given to the group of exciting young players signed by the manager Matt Busby. Charlton remained faithful to Manchester United for his entire career.

The Busby Babes seemed destined to become one of the finest club teams the world had seen, but tragically the heart of the team was killed by an air crash at Munich airport on their way back to England after a European Cup match in February 1958. Eight players, three officials, and eight journalists died in the disaster.

Bobby Charlton was the link between that great team and the next great Manchester United team. He made his first appearance for England in 1958 and played a crucial role in England's reemergence as a world soccer power in the 1960s, playing alongside players like Banks, Moore, and Greaves.

Charlton had started out as an attacker, but he soon developed a deeper-lying role from which he could make devastating runs or deliver long, accurate passes. This role was very demanding, but Charlton's athleticism and will to win were equal to it. And these qualities were evident for all to see in England's finest hour—the 1966 World Cup Finals.

In their opening game England had been held to a goalless draw by the defensive tactics of Uruguay. In England's second match, Mexico adopted similar tactics, challenging the hosts to take the initiative. The crowd was getting restless when Charlton collected the ball in his own half, beat two defenders, and unleashed a fierce right-footed shot that gave Calderon, the Mexican goal-keeper, no chance. Charlton also had a hand in England's second goal, with a great defense-splitting pass to Greaves, whose shot rebounded for Hunt to score. Those two incidents restored England's faith in their team.

In the semifinal, England met Portugal, and once again Charlton gave an exhibition of scoring. His first was side-footed from 20 yards, and his second was hit on the run with such power and accuracy that even the Portuguese players applauded the Manchester United star. Charlton's role in the final was somewhat cancelled out by Franz Beckenbauer but, by the same token, it did not allow the young German to have such an influential role either. To cap a memorable year, Charlton was named European Footballer of the Year.

Manchester United had won the league title in 1965 and repeated the feat in 1967. The following year, Charlton captained them to European Cup glory, scoring twice in their historic victory over Benfica and becoming the first British club to win the trophy. The combination of Charlton, George Best, and Denis Law still evoke wonderful memories for all those who saw United play in their heyday.

In the 1970 World Cup finals England had struggled through its opening group and faced West Germany in the quarterfinal. Charlton was playing a record 106th cap for his country, and all seemed to be going well when they went 2–0 ahead. Beckenbauer reduced the deficit and shortly after this, Alf Ramsey, the English manager, took off Charlton. Although he was tiring, many thought that this was a tactical mistake, as such was Charlton's influence over his team and opponents that it could only have given the Germans fresh heart. No doubt the point will be debated endlessly, but West Germany went on to win the match. This marked Charlton's final game for his country—a disappointing end to England's most-capped player and record goal scorer.

Charlton bowed out at Old Trafford in April 1973 after scoring 247 goals in 754 games. In 1984 he joined the United board, combining his work with soccer schools for youngsters. He is still one of the game's finest ambassadors.

His finishing apart, Bobby Charlton will always be remembered for his powerful running and sudden bursts of acceleration that enabled him to swerve away from opponents at speed before switching the direction of attack with an accurate long pass.

MICHEL PLATINI

The French national team of the 1980s was one of the most artistic and talented sides to have ever graced the World Cup finals. They were also one of the unluckiest. In Spain in 1982 and again four years in Mexico, they deserved a place in the final, but were beaten by West Germany on both occasions.

Although the team included such talented players as Jean Tigana, Alain Giresse, Dominique Rocheteau, and Marius Tresor, the linchpin who exemplified the true artistry and flair of French football was Michel Platini.

Born in 1955, Platini began his career in 1972 at Nancy, his hometown club, where his father was the coach. In 175 appearances Platini scored 98 league goals, including one against Nice that won the French Cup. After seven years he was bought by St. Etienne before moving to Italian giant Juventus in 1982 for $1.8 million.

Platini had made his international debut in 1976 and represented his country in the 1978 World Cup finals. France did not get past the first round, but made significant progress in 1982 to reach the semifinals against West Germany. The Germans took the lead, but with Platini in sparkling form an equalizer was always likely. France was awarded a penalty. Before placing the ball on the spot, Platini kissed it and then fired it home. The game went into extra time, and the French scored twice, seemingly on their way to the final. Perhaps the French should have consolidated their lead, or perhaps they lacked the resilience of the Germans, who scored twice to tie the game. In the penalty shoot-out that followed, Bossis fired his shot at the German goalkeeper, and the French were out.

Two years later in the European Championship, France demonstrated that they were the best team in Europe, if not the world. For Platini the tournament was a great personal triumph that elevated his reputation to that of players like Pele, Cruyff, and Beckenbauer. He scored nine goals in the five games, including one of his special curling free kicks, a skill gained by years of practice in swerving shots around a wall of wooden dummies.

In the same year, Platini won the second of three successive European Footballer of the Year awards and the first of two World Footballer of the Year titles. He was enjoying great success with Juventus in Italy and in European club competitions, all of which guaranteed him recognition as a world-class player.

But the time of the 1986 World Cup finals, the French team was reaching its peak. Platini had confirmed his status as one of the best players in the world, and it was his goal that defeated reigning champion Italy. In the next round the French faced Brazil in what turned out to be one of the most entertaining games in World Cup history. Brazil took the lead, but again Platini was on hand to coolly slot the ball home for the equalizer. The game went to extra time and penalties, and although Platini missed his spot kick, the French won through to the semifinals.

Drained by their efforts and the 100-degree heat of the classic quarterfinal, France could not lift its game against West Germany and once again failed to reach the final.

Platini retired the following year after winning 72 games for France and scoring a record 41 goals. He was appointed manager of the French national team but resigned after a disappointing European Championship finals in 1992.

WORLD CUP RECORDS

The first World Cup goal was scored by Lucien Laurent for France after 19 minutes against Mexico in 1930.

•

Frenchman Juste Fontaine scored a record 13 goals in six matches in the 1958 finals.

•

Gerd Muller scored 10 goals for West Germany in 1970 and four goals in 1974, for the highest aggregate of 14 goals.

•

Jairzinho (Brazil) scored seven goals in six games in 1970. The only other player to score in every match in a finals is Alcide Ghiggia of Uruguay, with four goals in four games in 1950.

•

Ramon Gonzales of Paraguay earned the dubious distinction of scoring the first own goal in a game against the United States in 1930.

•

Guillermo Stabile scored the first hat trick, for Argentina against Mexico in 1930. England's Geoff

Hurst is the only player to score a hat trick in a World Cup final. He scored three of England's four against West Germany.

•

The highest number of goals scored in a World Cup tournament is 140 in 1954 (average 5.38 per game). Austria's 7-5 victory certainly helped toward the total.

•

The highest number of goals scored by one team is 27 by Hungary in 1954. It was little consolation for not winning the final, though.

•

England scored just 27 seconds into their opening match against France in 1982. Bryan Robson's goal beat the previous record by three seconds.

•

The record margin of victory in a World Cup final tournament is nine goals: Hungary 10 El Salvador 1 (1982); Hungary 9 South Korea 0 (1954); Yugoslavia 9 Zaire 0 (1954). The highest aggregate is 12: Austria 7 Switzerland 5 (1954).

•

Nearly 200,000 people packed into the Maracana stadium in Rio for the 1950 final between Brazil and Uruguay, though only 150,000 tickets had been sold.

•

There have been two battles: The Battle of Berne in 1954 between Brazil and Hungary, and The Battle of Santiago between Chile and Italy in 1962.

•

Peru was the first winner of FIFA's Fair Play award, with no cautions in the 1970 finals.

•

Brazil became the first country to win the World Cup

final three times and earned the right to keep the Jules
Rimet Trophy.

●

Brazil was unbeaten in 13 consecutive World Cup
matches between 1958 and 1966, winning 11 and
drawing two. They were finally beaten, 3-1, by
Hungary. Italy holds the record for most successive
wins, with seven between 1934 and 1938.

●

At the age of 17 years and 41 days, Norman Whiteside
of Northern Ireland became the youngest-ever player
in the finals when he played against Yugoslavia in the
1978 finals.

●

Dino Zoff became the oldest player, at 40, to win a
World Cup winners' medal when he captained Italy to
their 1982 success.

●

Peru's captain, Mario de las Casas, earned the unwel-
come distinction of being the first player to be sent off
in a game against Romania in 1930.

DAY BY DAY :
YOUR PERSONAL
TOURNAMENT GRID

GROUP A
USA, SWITZERLAND, COLOMBIA, ROMANIA

GROUP B
CAMEROON, SWEDEN, BRAZIL, RUSSIA

GROUP C
GERMANY, BOLIVIA, SPAIN, SOUTH KOREA

GROUP D
ARGENTINA, GREECE, NIGERIA, BULGARIA

GROUP E
ITALY, REPUBLIC OF IRELAND, NORWAY,
MEXICO

GROUP F
BELGIUM, MOROCCO, HOLLAND, SAUDI ARABIA

	FIRST ROUND	**WINNER**

JUNE

17
Group C: GERMANY VS. BOLIVIA
(Chicago) _____
Group C: SPAIN VS. SOUTH KOREA
(Dallas) _____

18
Group A: UNITED STATES VS. SWITZERLAND
(Detroit) _____
Group A: COLOMBIA VS. ROMANIA
(Los Angeles) _____
Group E: ITALY VS. REPUBLIC OF IRELAND
(New York) _____

19
Group B: CAMEROON VS. SWEDEN
(Los Angeles) _____
Group E: NORWAY VS. MEXICO
(Washington, D.C.) _____
Group F: BELGIUM VS. MOROCCO
(Orlando) _____

20
Group B: BRAZIL VS. RUSSIA
(San Francisco) _____
Group F: HOLLAND VS. SAUDI ARABIA
(Washington, D.C.) _____

21
Group C: GERMANY VS. SPAIN
(Chicago) _____
Group D: ARGENTINA VS. GREECE
(Boston) _____
Group D: NIGERIA VS. BULGARIA
(Dallas) _____

22
Group A: UNITED STATES VS. COLOMBIA
(Los Angeles) _____
Group A: SWITZERLAND VS. ROMANIA
(Detroit) _____

23
Group C: BOLIVIA VS. SOUTH KOREA
(Boston) _____
Group E: ITALY VS. NORWAY
(New York) _____

24 **Group B:** BRAZIL VS. CAMEROON
(San Francisco) _____
Group B: RUSSIA VS. SWEDEN
(Detroit) _____
Group E: REPUBLIC OF IRELAND VS. MEXICO
(Orlando) _____

25 **Group D:** ARGENTINA VS. NIGERIA
(Boston) _____
Group F: BELGIUM VS. HOLLAND
(Orlando) _____
Group F: MOROCCO VS. SAUDI ARABIA
(New York) _____

26 **Group A:** UNITED STATES VS. ROMANIA
(Los Angeles) _____
Group A: SWITZERLAND VS. COLOMBIA
(San Francisco) _____
Group D: GREECE VS. BULGARIA
(Chicago) _____

27 **Group C:** GERMANY VS. SOUTH KOREA
(Dallas) _____
Group C: BOLIVIA VS. SPAIN
(Chicago) _____

28 **Group B:** BRAZIL VS. SWEDEN
(Detroit) _____
Group B: RUSSIA VS. CAMEROON
(San Francisco) _____
Group E: ITALY VS. MEXICO
(Washington, D.C.) _____
Group E: REPUBLIC OF IRELAND VS. NORWAY
(New York) _____

29 **Group F:** BELGIUM VS. SAUDI ARABIA
(Washington, D.C.) _____
Group F: MOROCCO VS. HOLLAND
(Orlando) _____

30 **Group D:** ARGENTINA VS. BULGARIA
(Dallas) _____
Group D: GREECE VS. NIGERIA
(Boston)

FIRST ROUND FINAL TABLES

Group A

POS	TEAM	P	W	D	L	F	A	Pts.
1								
2								
3								
4								

Group B

POS	TEAM	P	W	D	L	F	A	Pts.
1								
2								
3								
4								

Group C

POS	TEAM	P	W	D	L	F	A	Pts.
1								
2								
3								
4								

Group D

POS	TEAM	P	W	D	L	F	A	Pts.
1								
2								
3								
4								

Group E

POS	TEAM	P	W	D	L	F	A	Pts.
1								
2								
3								
4								

Group F

POS	TEAM	P	W	D	L	F	A	Pts.
1								
2								
3								
4								

SECOND ROUND

Game 37: (Chicago)
GROUP C WINNER
VS.
A, B OR F 3RD PLACE

_____

_____

Winner: _____

Game 38: (Washington, D.C.)
GROUP A 2ND PLACE
VS.
C 2ND PLACE

_____

_____

Winner: _____

Game 39: (Dallas)
GROUP F 2ND PLACE
VS.
B 2ND PLACE

_____

_____

Winner: _____

Game 40: (Los Angeles)
GROUP A WINNER
VS.
C, D OR E 3RD PLACE

_____

_____

Winner: _____

Game 41: (Orlando)
GROUP F WINNER
VS.
E 2ND PLACE

_____

_____

Winner: _____

Game 42: (San Francisco)
GROUP B WINNER
VS.
A, C OR D 3RD PLACE

_____

_____

Winner: _____

5

Game 43: (Boston)
GROUP D WINNER _____
VS.
B, E OR F 3RD PLACE _____

Winner: _____

Game 44: (New York)
GROUP E WINNER _____
VS.
D 2ND PLACE _____

Winner: _____

QUARTERFINALS

9

Game 45: (Boston)
GAME 43 WINNER _____
VS.
GAME 38 WINNER _____

Winner: _____

Game 46: (Dallas)
GAME 41 WINNER _____
VS.
GAME 42 WINNER _____

Winner: _____

10

Game 47: (New York)
GAME 44 WINNER _____
VS.
GAME 37 WINNER _____

Winner: _____

Game 48: (San Francisco)
GAME 39 WINNER _____
VS.
GAME 40 WINNER _____

Winner: _____

SEMIFINALS

13 **Game 49:** (New York)
GAME 47 WINNER
_____
VS.
GAME 45 WINNER
_____

Winner: _____

Game 50: (Los Angeles)
GAME 48 WINNER
_____
VS.
GAME 46 WINNER
_____

Winner: _____

THIRD-PLACE PLAY-OFF

16 **Game 51:** (Los Angeles)
SEMIFINAL LOSER
_____
VS.
SEMIFINAL LOSER
_____

Winner: _____

FINAL

17 **Game 52:** (Los Angeles)
SEMIFINAL WINNER
_____
VS.
SEMIFINAL WINNER
_____

Winner: _____

WORLD CUP CHAMPIONS '94

_____

ABOUT THE AUTHORS

Anybody who's anybody knows about the size of Glen Phillips's database. It's huge and getting bigger. As a researcher and writer of sports and contemporary music, updating information and going to all-night parties is a full-time job for him.

He was born in London, England in the '50s and now lives on the southeast coast of England with his unlawfully beautiful wife, Pip, and their children, Edward and April. He is currently working on a project to turn cricket into the number one sport in the USA.

From biology graduate to sports editor, Tim Oldham has taken a somewhat unusual route to sports journalism. As editor of the successful series of BBC Sports magazines, he was responsible for preview titles for such diverse sporting occasions as World Cup '90, Wimbledon, the Grand Prix season, and golf's major tournaments.